DISCARD

Citizen Participation
and
Public Library Policy

by
JANE ROBBINS

The Scarecrow Press, Inc.
Metuchen, N. J.   1975

Library of Congress Cataloging in Publication Data

Robbins, Jane, 1939-
    Citizen participation and public library policy.

    Bibliography: p.
    Includes index.
    1.   Public libraries--United States--Administration--
Citizen participation.   I.   Title.
Z678. R62   025. 1   74-34248
ISBN 0-8108-0796-3

TABLE OF CONTENTS

LIST OF TABLES

v

LIST OF FIGURES

PREFACE

During the late 1950's and early 1960's some of the early empirical research of social scientists began to be noticed by persons in policy and program decision-making positions within both the private and public arena. The theoretical works of Weber, Durkheim and many others had been considered previously, but it was not until social science began to gather to itself the aura of a "real" or "hard" science that its propositions were actually taken seriously by decision-makers.

This new legitimacy of the social sciences (whose studies had indicated failures and inconsistencies in American society, e.g., poverty in the midst of affluence), coupled with a certain freedom to "experiment" born of economic prosperity, plus an uneasy feeling about the future capacity of urban man to control his environment (to say nothing of controlling himself), led to new ways in which to address contemporary societal problems. Notwithstanding Daniel Moynihan's well-received remark that "the role of social science lies not in the formulation of social policy, but in the measurement of its results,"[1] the moment was ripe for the influence of social science theory, regardless of whether it was well-substantiated, to lead policy and program formulation.

Some viewed this development as unethical experimentation on unknowing publics, with large sums of other persons' monies, in pursuit of unknown goals; but, others saw it as a

welcome, necessary and valid step toward social change.
This latter group felt that there was as much "factual" background to support new policies as there ever had been for
the past social policies which had been charted and pursued
in America. Any change was needed, for it seemed that the
past policies had exacerbated rather than relieved societal
malaise. [2]

Thus, during the past decade a new approach to the
problems of community life began to take shape and evolve
into test implementations. This new approach called for a
reappraisal of the problems to be attacked; the priority was
to lay foundations for the development of a cohesive community life style by concentrating on the attitudes of the community residents rather than on the development of the physical and functional aspects of the community.

One justification for this approach was based upon the
reported inroads made by the Ford Foundation-sponsored Public Affairs Program. Ford was the first foundation to support community organizations with large amounts of money. [3]
The programs sponsored by Ford were known as the "grey
areas projects." They were unabashedly attempts to transform the political and social life of communities through effective community organization. The reasons for attempting
this new approach were outlined by Paul N. Ylvisaker, the
head of the Public Affairs Program:

(1)   a systems analytical approach to community
      problems is essential;

(2)   it is necessary to capitalize on the new feel-
      ings of self-respect to be found among com-
      munity residents;

(3)   processes in the social system can be per-
      fected through various devices discovered
      through social science research; and

(4)   social innovations cannot be expected to arise
out of existing community agencies.[4]

In 1961 the National Institutes of Mental Health, along
with support from the Ford Foundation and the City of New
York, initiated the Mobilization for Youth Project (MFY).
MFY was profoundly influenced by the work of Richard Cloward and Lloyd Ohlin of the Columbia School of Social Work.
Their research into the causes of juvenile delinquency reduced the role of individual pathology to one of minimal influence and identified the major cause as lack of actual and/
or perceived equal economic and educational opportunity.[5]
MFY was one of the first federal projects undertaken to be
based upon opportunity theory.[6]

The election of John F. Kennedy and the subsequent
introduction of his administration-wide New Frontier programs
(initiated under Lyndon Johnson's War on Poverty) brought
additional federal commitment to the nurturing of community
life.   The formula read: increase opportunities, add an em-
phasis on planning, coordinate efforts in concerned public
and private sectors and improvement in community life will
result; however, the opening of the avenues to opportunity
was not to be simply achieved for there was a concomitant
necessity.   The opportunities made available must be perceived to be relevant to the lives of those for whom they
were intended.   In order to allow perception to take place,
the frustration and alienation of community residents had to
be overcome.   And so, to the formula for the development
of community life, the ingredient of citizen participation was
added.

The formula was crystallized in the programs funded
under the Economic Opportunity Act of 1964 (EOA) and the
Demonstration Cities and Metropolitan Development Act of

1966 (Model Cities Act). Both of these Acts made explicit requirements for citizen participation: EOA called it "maximum feasible participation"[7] and the Model Cities Act required "wide-spread citizen participation."[8] The policy requirement was evident, but its intent and the means for implementation of the policy were not. The ambiguity of the citizen participation requirements laid the foundation for much of the controversy and conflict which followed. On the one hand, the ambiguity opened a wedge into the existing community political power structures for those citizen groups and their advocates who considered political powerlessness and feelings of inefficacy and alienation toward the existent political structure to be the major factors perpetuating cyclical poverty and pathological behaviors; on the other hand, the ambiguity allowed the existing political structure to interpret the participation clauses as mere platitudes.

By the time the Model Cities Act was passed in 1966, the embrace on citizen participation had already lessened, and by 1967, when the Economic Opportunity Act came up for continuance in Congress, citizen participation was suffering the pain of "premature" rejection. The 1968 national elections brought the introduction of a new administration which had made clear its opposition to citizen participation. The Washington Post of May 3, 1971 ran a first-page story with the headline, "End of Programs Run by Poor Foreseen under Nixon Proposal." The article cited several Office of Economic Opportunity programs which had been disbanded and stated that the Nixon administration is "opposed to giving funds to agencies that battle with regularly elected officials."[9]

The EOA and Model Cities Act have been extended since the years of their enactment. Senate Bill 2007, to authorize continued funds for the Office of Economic Opportunity, was sent to the President for signature into Law, December 8, 1971. Yet, even though citizen boards still exist, the financial and ideological commitment which was evident at their inception has been lost.

During the same period which saw the birth of the Economic Opportunity and Model Cities Acts, specific library legislation was also being enacted. Between the provisions of the EOA, Model Cities Act, Library Services and Construction Act (P. L. 89-511) and Elementary and Secondary Education Act (P. L. 89-10), opportunities for libraries to involve themselves in new community programs were great. Titles I, II and VII of the Model Cities Act make specific references to libraries and, although no specific provision for library participation appeared in the EOA, Titles I, II and VIII definitely include opportunities for library involvement.

If the quest for community is as pervasive in the United States today as many social scientists believe it to be,[10] and if, as they contend, that search must be "armed with information,"[11] then the American public library is a natural partner in that quest.

Throughout its history the American public library has claimed that its services are available and provided to all persons across the societal spectrum. Although the democracy of its service delivery has been challenged, it is for the most part only recently that the democracy of its decision-making processes has been directly scrutinized.[12] Is the public library's decision-making structure participative and is its policy-making process receptive to inputs by citizens? Further, are the service goals of libraries which include citizen input in the decision-making process different from libraries which do not include citizen input? These are the questions which promoted this study.

Acknowledgments

The responsibility for the study rests with the author, but throughout its development many persons made substantial contributions. My doctoral student colleagues often encouraged me to continue investigating the elusive questions from which my concern emanated. They provided essential constructive criticism, especially during the sample design and questionnaire construction stages. I am especially grateful to Mr. Peter T. Westphal for his aid during the tedious coding and keypunching phase and also to the Computer Science Center, University of Maryland through which computer time was provided. My greatest debt of thanks is owed to the more than 165 librarians who took time to complete the questionnaire or in some other way took part in the survey; also I wish to thank heartily all who were so kind and helpful to me at the case study site. Sincere thanks go to my advisor, Dr. Edwin E. Olson, who knows so well when to encourage and when to criticize. And finally, I wish to thank the American taxpayer, who through the Higher Education Act, Title II-B, supported me while I pursued this study.

Jane Robbins
Pittsburgh, Pennsylvania

Notes

1. Daniel P. Moynihan, Maximum Feasible Misunderstanding (New York: Free Press, 1970), p. 193.

2. For example, the 1954 Amendment to the Housing Act of 1949, which provided funds for urban renewal, was met with active and often violent resistance by many.

3. Moynihan, op. cit., p. 35.

4. Ibid., p. 40-41.

5. Richard A. Cloward and Lloyd E. Ohlin, Delinquency and Opportunity: A Theory of Delinquent Gangs (New York: Free Press, 1960).

6. This project was one of the few which dared to risk antagonizing its sponsoring, as well as other public agencies; it disastrously miscalculated its power to gain concessions from those who controlled it.

7. U. S. Laws, Statutes, etc., Economic Opportunity Act of 1964 (P. L. 88-452) (Washington, D. C.: Government Printing Office, 1964), Title II-A, Section 202 (a) (3).

8. U. S. Laws, Statutes, etc., Demonstration Cities and Metropolitan Development Act of 1966 (P. L. 89-754) (Washington, D. C.: Government Printing Office, 1966), Title I-A, Section 103(a) (2).

9. The Washington Post, May 3, 1971, p. 1.

10. For example, see the collection of essays in Willis D. Hawley and Frederick M. Wirt, The Search for Community Power (Englewood Cliffs, N. J.: Prentice-Hall, 1968).

11. Moynihan, op. cit., p. xxv. (From a statement of the Board of Directors of the National Association for Community Development.)

12. Many in the field date the beginning of the scrutiny to 1969, when the Congress for Change (Washington, D. C.) and the Annual Meeting of the American Library Association (Atlantic City, N. J.) brought concern for participatory democracy in libraries and within the Association itself to the forefront of deliberations; however, the classical study of the library's political environment, Oliver Garceau's The Public Library in the Political Process (New York: Columbia University Press, 1949), has implication in the area of participatory decision-making.

Chapter 1

INTRODUCTION:
THEORETICAL FOUNDATIONS

The purpose of this chapter is to explicate the issues, both theoretical and operational, which surround the concept of citizen participation. No new conceptual definition is proffered, nor are new categories of objectives for citizen participation processes identified; rather, this is a review of what I find to be the most compelling treatments of the concept by a variety of sociologists, political scientists and planners. Further, it 'contains a statement of my view as to what conclusions may tentatively be drawn from the numerous theoretical and empirical studies which bear upon the concept.

The first section deals with what is perhaps the most fundamental aspect of the citizen participation question; i.e., the philosophical tradition which acts to bolster the acceptance of the concept as essential to the perpetuation of American political democracy. The next section treats citizen participation as a process pursuant of a myriad of distinct and definable objectives. Because citizen participation in American society is at once a conceptual construct fundamental to democratic tradition and a process whereby that concept can be realized, it is well to examine these aspects of participation separately and then to fit them together into the dynamic whole which is more explanatory of its essence. The third section focuses upon two elusive but critical concepts which

1

play roles in the realization of participatory democracy.
The first, poverty culture, is a relatively new concept applicable to political situations; the second, power structure,
is important to an understanding of all political arenas.   The
final section of the chapter wrestles with what the preceding
discussion appears to mean in terms of what role citizen
participation plays in contemporary society and what research
objectives social scientists might best pursue in order to gain
a fuller and more tractable understanding of the citizen participation phenomenon.

The Concept of Citizen Participation

Political philosophers from Aristotle down through
John Dewey and on to Amitai Etzioni have touted participation
as everything from the means by which the full range of
knowledge within society can be activated to a defense against
tyranny.   Participation can simultaneously be the impetus to
change within society and the promoter of its order and sta-
bility.   In addition to its grand effects upon the collective
society, it further has the capacity to ennoble men by giving
them a sense of personal value and dignity.   It can promote
a shared sense of responsibility for the welfare of the State
between the rulers and the ruled.

While participation is extolled for its virtues, there
is disagreement over how open or closed participation should
be.   For various reasons, most often religious, racial or
moral, many have suggested that not all members of society
are equally worthy of being political participants.   Thus the
question becomes not simply a theoretical one, bound to the
practice of democracy (participation is often more valued in
totalitarian societies for its legitimizing properties), but also

an operational one.   Participation, yes; but by whom?

The concern over who should participate in politics in
American society has increased considerably during the last
century.   Although there is still debate over who actually has
a stake in society, and most recently, as expressed by such
Freudian New-left philosophers as Paul Goodman and Herbert
Marcuse, over who would even want a stake in contemporary
American society, the present arguments favoring limited
participation emphasize society's increased technical and structural complexity.   It is not that all do not share in the impact of political decision-making and thus should have the
right to participate, but rather than being able to comprehend
or imagine those impacts is within the capacities of only the
most highly-informed and sensitive few.   Running counter to
this argument is one which also acknowledges the increased
complexities of contemporary society, but as opposed to lim-
iting decision-making to the few, it calls for a reorganization
of society into smaller units which would be characterized by
high-levels of participation in decision-making affecting local
life-style components such as public safety, education and libraries, while leaving system-maintenance functions such as
garbage collection and pollution control to larger decision-
making units. [1]

During the past four decades there has been considerable empirical research into the political behavior of man.
Much of this research has been limited in scope, but it has
begun to create a tenuous, although relatively "factual" picture of political behavior.   Perhaps the major conclusions
which can be drawn that relate to the issues of this study
are: 1) patterns of political behavior are fluid and change
with relation to candidates, issues, and the background of
the participants.   Rarely are participation rates as high as

two-thirds of those eligible.   This two-thirds figure relates
to avowed political interest, not actual political interest;
and, 2) political participation is a <u>learned</u> behavior.

     At the present time, the primary area of concern in
political participation research is upon non-participants.
Non-participants appear to fall into two groups, the apathetic
and the alienated.   In simplistic terms, apathetics are those
who disdain politics for various reasons.   One group of
apathetics which has been afforded notice of late are the
branch of the "hippies" who have dropped out of contemporary society.   They are those who should, according to socio-
economic variables which correlate with participation, be
part of the small "attentive public. "[2]   The other group of
non-participants is the alienated; i. e., those persons who
have the right to participate but do not because of feelings
of inefficacy and/or mystification.   These alienated persons
are characterized by their lack of education and isolation
from the "mainstream" of society, in social, economic, psy-
chological and political terms.   The larger part of the research in non-participation has focused its concern on the
alienated.   Much of this research has taken the form of
analyses and/or evaluations of projects planned and implemented under the Economic Opportunity Act of 1964 and the
Demonstration Cities and Metropolitan Development Act of
1966, popularly known as the Model Cities Act.   This research clearly indicates that citizen participation is indeed
a powerful concept, but is one which is open to many inter-
pretations depending upon what objective is to be met by
means of the process.

     As a concept, citizen participation has become re-
ified in our society; reified in its formal sociological sense;
i. e., as an institutionalization that has lost its origin as a

man-constructed concept and has become a given, a non-
or supra-human dispensation.   As Edmund Burke so simply
states it: "Citizens should share in decisions affecting their
destinies."[3]   Murray Edelman makes the point even more
explicitly.   Belief in participatory democracy is reified in
part because it is not empirically demonstrable that this is,
or is not, in fact the way government works in this country
or how management decisions are made.   This is what
Americans want to believe and thus seek.   The symbol of
participatory democracy thus serves as a part of the ma-
chinery of system maintenance by acting as a simplification
in a dismayingly complex situation.[4]

Citizen participation in American society is a major
thread of its fabric, and is therefore self-justifying.   As a
conceptual tool it is weak because it can take unto itself any
number of attributes--all in pursuit of one righteous, but un-
defined, goal.   In order to make it a meaningful concept,
its attributes must be identified and the goals which it pur-
sues must be explicated.

The Process of Citizen Participation

Perhaps the major reason citizen participation is such
a compelling concept is that it serves so many purposes so
uncompromisingly; however, in order to have meaningful
programs which include citizen input, the goals which are
to be met via the process must be fully communicated and
understood by all the actors.[5]   In a sense what is called
for is a systems analytic approach to each specific project
which calls for citizen participation in order to determine:
1) the effective citizen participation goal in terms of the
statement of the problem; 2) the "hard and soft" resources

available; 3) the time-frame; and 4) the statement of objectives. Even if the actual intent of the project is to be in
some way protected from full communication, the most
salient actors in the program must be so advised and a
sense of camaraderie must be developed within the project.

Many categorizations of the citizen participation process have emerged out of the several hundred studies of
Community Action (Title II of the Economic Opportunity Act)
and Model Cities programs that have been undertaken. A
series of other secondary writers have in turn analyzed
these categorizations and have attempted to classify them.
This classification has most often resulted in a dichotomized
scheme. For example, the Brandeis University study mentions organizational and/or political goals; Clark and Hopkins distinguish between community organization and/or community action in much the same sense; and Jack Rothman
proffers a dichotomous scheme of "particularized problems
in function, " i.e., organizational goals and/or "general capacity to function, " i.e., political goals. [6] It appears that
the dichotomous classification is a sound one, for the citizen
participation process as it has been put into action in poverty programs has pursued one or the other (or both) of
these two relatively distinct objectives. However, because
a significant number of projects have been reported in which
various strategies appear to be pursuing both goals simultaneously, the development of a multifarious or continuum
concept of the goals might well be more illustrative and of
greater explanatory power in characterizing the actual behaviors of groups utilizing citizen participation in decision-
making. A possible typological presentation of citizen participation processes follows:

I. SERVICE-ORIENTED GOALS/ORGANIZATION
    MAINTENANCE

    A. Citizens as Communications Links between
        Program Planners and Program Beneficiaries.
        1. Information; for purposes of explaining
            programs and responding to inquiries.
        2. Consultation; for purposes of eliciting
            consent from those effected.
        3. Negotiation; for purposes of eliciting ad-
            vice from those affected.

    B. Citizens as Employees in the Program.
        1. Social Integration; for purposes of legiti-
            mization.
        2. Social Mobility; for purposes of aiding the
            few via the project.

II. INDIVIDUAL-THERAPY GOALS/SYSTEM MAIN-
     TENANCE

    A. Education.
        1. For purposes of learning how bureauc-
            racy works.
        2. For purposes of learning problem solv-
            ing techniques.
        3. For purposes of political socialization to
            the existing state of affairs.

    B. Psychological therapy.
        1. For purposes of developing feeling of
            personal and corporate efficacy.
        2. For purposes of developing self-confi-
            dence, self-reliance, i.e., create the
            psychological capacity for the citizen to
            want to help himself.

III. POLITICAL-ORIENTATION GOALS/SYSTEM
      CHANGE

    A. Internally directed.
        1. Political involvement by existing groups.
        2. Development of new political groups.
        3. In-fighting between local groups over
            access to formal representation positions.

    B. Externally directed.

1. Impact the existing power structure.
2. Share with the existing power structure.
3. Change the existing power structure.
4. Destroy the existing power structure.

The above typology deals only with the substantive dimension of citizen participation, i. e., the domain of action. Other important dimensions of citizen participation are: 1) representative, i. e., the arrangements which establish the way in which participants are selected; and 2) descriptive, i. e., the degree to which participants actually reflect the characteristics of their constituents. [7] Empirical studies focusing upon these two latter dimensions indicate that they tend to influence the substantive dimension;[8] however, for the purposes of this chapter it is the substantive/action, or output dimension that is of concern.

Whether or not citizen participation is fundamentally a dichotomous, trichotomous or multifarious process, [9] it seems clear that at this stage,

> every effort to reduce its protean-like substance
> to a definable, systematic, and comprehensible
> body of thought is resisted by inherent dilemmas--
> contradictions between myth and reality and even
> between different sets of observable social phenom-
> ena. Citizen participation virtually defies general-
> ization and delights in reducing abstractions to
> dust. [10]

The only "answer" to solving these dilemmas seems to be the development of a still larger body of empirical research from which more meaningful inferences may be drawn.

Ralph Kramer, [11] in his study of five Community Action Programs in California, views citizen participation as a strategy in much the same manner as Burke; i. e., as more a response to environmental contingencies than as a response to value premises. He suggests that the greater a citizen participation organization's capacity to concentrate power and create coalitions, whether strictly political or bureaucratic and professional, the more likely there will be conflict in the program. He seems to assume that there is 1) an inherent dissension between program initiators and proposed program "beneficiaries," (this dissension may be based upon either value or interest differences; and 2) that this dissension will come to the forefront dependent upon the resources for influence at the disposal of the beneficiary groups. (Whether in fact there are value as well as interest differences between these two groups is examined below.)

Some support for Kramer's hypothesis that the coalition formation capability within a citizen group is a key resource within the community decision-making arena is afforded by Michael Lipsky. Lipsky contends that citizen participation groups which have power resources of their own can engage in direct confrontation with some "hope" of gaining access to the decision-making arena or some other desired reward, either substantive or symbolic; however, "relatively powerless groups" must form alliances in order to gain the rewards which they seek. The spark which ignites alliance formation must either come from an indigenous leader (hard to find among the poor?) or from a community advocate (suspicious character?).[12]

Studies such as those cited above show the degree to which participation by traditionally non-participating citizens is a political problem, not only in a philosophical context, but also in an operational one. Although the avowed intent of poverty programs is to do something about economic conditions, as Richard Cloward states it, "Economic deprivation is fundamentally a political problem."[13] If one is in-

clined to view economic and social policy as largely an out-
growth of political policy, then the pursuit of solely service-
oriented or individual/therapy goals seems to be pursuit of
objectives that skirt, confuse or obliterate the fundamental
issue. From this point of view (which I admit to holding)
it appears that all citizen participation strategies that have
been identified are essentially political:

    (1) service-oriented goals are designed to maintain
           the local political structure and its public service
           bureaucracies as they now function with only mi-
           nor concessions to participating citizens. This
           is the least that must be done to bolster the pop-
           ular belief in a democratic heritage.

    (2) individual/therapy goals tend more to an open
           acknowledgment of the "politics" of the situation,
           but avoid the issue by claiming that participants
           must first be "cured" of their non-participatory
           mind-set.

The pursuit of political goals in a community development project must be carefully analyzed to determine whether
the political action is internally or externally focused. Internal political activity involves competition within the target
population for recognition as the legitimate representative of
the population. The competition may be instigated by those
basically interested in maintaining the larger embedding
political power structure or may be promoted by those who
wish to use political "games" for their therapeutic or in-
structional value.

Those persons who maintain that the only effective
goal of community development programs is the restructuring of the present power structure (often classified as community control advocates) delight in the few projects which
have entered into external political confrontation. Even if
there is no "change, " at least the dissension has been brought

out into the open. Confrontation has forced the existing
power group to impose sanctions; thus its legitimacy has
been challenged or at least its vulnerability has been ex-
posed. The discontinuance of many of the projects which
have openly confronted existing power structures has been
used to provide evidence in support of E. E. Schattschneider's concept of the "mobilization of bias."[14] Although the
discontinuance of projects may be a pleasing symbolic reward for the participating citizens, it seems rather shallow
considering the substantive needs of various commities or,
often more accurately, the substantive needs of the communities which the participating group is supposed to represent.

The realization of participatory democracy, especially
in political arenas characterized by the high incidence of
"low-status" constituents, is problematical. Two related
theoretical concepts which tend to make citizen participation
highly difficult to control conceptually are: 1) the culture of
poverty, and 2) power. This chapter now turns to a discussion of these two concepts.

Culture of Poverty and Power Structure

The clearest recent explication of the culture of poverty concept is to be found in Edward C. Banfield's The Unheavenly City.

> The lower-class forms of all problems are at
> bottom a single problem: the existence of an out-
> look and style of life which is radically present-
> oriented and which therefore attaches no value to
> work, sacrifice, self-improvement, or service to
> family, friends, or community. Social workers,
> teachers, and law-enforcement officials--all of
> those whom Gans calls 'caretakers'--cannot achieve
> their goals because they can neither change nor
> circumvent this cultural obstacle. [15]

What Banfield is doing in this book is expanding upon the
concept of the "private-regarding ethos" which he and James
Q. Wilson advanced in the early 1960's. Those who have
the private-regarding ethos are characterized by: 1) a
limited time perspective; 2) difficulty in abstracting from
concrete experiences; 3) unfamiliarity with and lack of confidence in city-wide institutions; 4) a preoccupation with the
personal and the immediate; and 5) few, if any, attachments
to organizations of any kind with the possible exception of
churches. [16]

    The key word in the quotation from The Unheavenly
City is "culturally." A culture, in the classical anthropo-
logical sense, is characterized by a self-supporting, on-
going system with a distinct design for living, principles of
organization and a system of values which is passed on to
the next generation through purposive socialization. The
concept of the culture of poverty arose in response to a
need for a framework within which the data and knowledge
relevant to poverty groups could be categorized and made
tractable. This extension of the concept of culture to the
explication of the characteristics of the poor is understandable, but is a misapplication of the formal concept. [17] The
main basis upon which poverty culture claims its validity is
empirical evidence of historical continuity, i. e., persistence,
of low-income behavior patterns. [18] One difficulty with this
contention is that most of the supporting studies have not
considered carefully or fully enough (if they did so at all)
the extent to which these low-income behavior patterns were
logical, rational responses to external pressures in society;
and more importantly, the extent to which these patterns are
purposefully passed on from one generation to the next. The
distinction to be made here is between what are cultures,

sub-cultures and classes in the sociological sense.

Elliot Liebow makes two important distinctions concerning the value system in lower-class life. First, Liebow states that the lower-class value system is derivative and subsidiary, and is weakly internalized, thus not having strong positive influence on behavior; and second, that it is not distinct, but rather appears in association with the parent value system and is separable from it only analytically.

> This inside world of low-income, urban, black males does not appear as a self-contained, self-generating, self-sustaining system or even sub-system with clear boundaries marking it off from the larger world around it. It is in continuous, intimate contact with the larger society--indeed, is an integral part of it--and is no more impervious to the values, sentiments and beliefs of the larger society than it is to the blue collar welfare agents of the larger society... [19]

> What appears as a dynamic, self-sustaining cultural process is, in part at least, a relatively simple piece of social machinery which turns out, in rather mechanical fashion, independently produced look-alikes. [20]

This non-cultural concept of low-status members of society views the lower-class as a heterogeneous sub-society which includes a variety of sub-cultures. In other words, the low-status group is a coherent collectivity within the larger society which shares with the larger society common cultural themes; between this lower-class society and the rest of society there exists multi-directional feedback on both societal and cultural dimensions. This view readily accepts that there are observable differences in life-styles and values, but focuses upon responses to external societal conditions rather than upon interpersonal characteristics.

The reason there has been so much controversy over

these two approaches to the problems of poverty is that they
indicate decidedly different objectives to be sought through
social policy. Those who hold to the culture of poverty view
feel that service, and certainly politically-oriented programs,
can be of no real impact unless the individual pathologies of
those caught in the culturally induced cycle of poverty are
cured. Banfield refers to this necessary process as
"middle-classifying" the poor. Supporters of societal causality for poverty state simply that "... sociotherapeutic intent ... is not germane to the people of the community!"[21]

Some recent significant value research appears to re-
fute the culture of poverty concept. One especially relevant
study on aspirational and terminal values was undertaken by
Rokeach and Parker. The study suggests that different
value systems do indeed distinguish the poor from the rich,
but not the black from the white. For example,

> Our data ... do not provide support for the wide-
> ly held belief that the culture of the poor is char-
> acterized by present-oriented, hedonistic values.
> We find no differences between the poor and the
> rich on an exciting life or on pleasure. Both of
> these values are ranked well toward the bottom of
> the terminal value scale by poor and rich alike.
> Moreover, the idea that the poor value immediate
> gratification more than the rich does not receive
> support from the NORC [National Opinion Research
> Center] data. There are no significant differences
> associated with income on self-controlled.

> It is also important to note that the value similar-
> ities and differences which we have described here
> as characterizing the poor and the rich are not to
> be thought of in a dichotomous way, but in terms
> of a continuum of status. Strictly speaking, it is
> not correct to speak of a 'culture of poverty' and
> a 'culture of affluence.' It would be more accu-
> rate to speak of variations of value systems asso-
> ciated with variations of status.[22]

The value which best distinguished the poor from the rich in this study was clean; the authors point out that one often values less what one already has than what one aspires to have. This one study does not, of course, indicate that the causal factors for poverty have been positively and solely traced to societal and/or organizational pathologies; it does, however, suggest that much research is still needed regarding the complex of causality relevant to poverty.

That there is an entrenched belief in the value of individual autonomy in this country seems to be clear. Since there is now evidence that society works in some instances to constrain individual liberty, it seems that research investigating the factors in society which tend to demoralize the poor should be supported. The research concerned with societal failures further suggests that it may indeed be profitable to look into the political structures in which poverty programs are embedded to find some of the causal factors associated with poverty. It appears that the poverty stricken need both politically-oriented programs in order to provide avenues into the existing political power structure and service programs to maintain them while they contend for power positions.

Many barriers to effective citizen participation have been proffered in the literature; e.g., need for long term, intense involvement; need for cosmopolitan rather than parochial efforts; lack of technical knowledge; lack of knowledge of the political milieu; lack of belief in the capacity of the system to be responsive to the needs of the poor, etc. There is evidence to support belief in each of these barriers. No one of them seems to be a unidimensional barrier, nor to stand unrelated to the others. For instance, with regard to the failure of the public service delivery system, one can

find a host of contingent failures and problems which play a
role. Michael Lipsky has suggested that one of the problems attached to service delivery arises at the level of face-
to-face contact between users of the public service system
and low-echelon or, using his term, "street-level" bureau-
crats. Lipsky contends, using policemen, school teachers
and lower court judges as examples, that the problems which
arise at this level of representing government to the people
are exacerbated by: 1) lack of organizational and personal
resources; 2) the presence of potential physical and psycho-
logical threat [multidirectional]; and 3) conflicting and ambiguous role expectations. [23]

    Granting that there are barriers toward citizen par-
ticipation of various kinds and intensities, the most difficult
barrier to contend with may be the structure of the political
system itself. During the last two decades a battle has
been raging among community power structure scholars; the
battle is both theoretical and methodological. Although the
methodological argument is indeed an important one, and
has keen implications for the theoretical one, for the purposes of this study only the theoretical aspects will be discussed. [24]

    The literature on community power is voluminous and
expanding with respect to both empirical studies and secondary analyses of those studies. In its most simple form, the
argument can be thought of as one between elitists and
pluralists. Elitists are represented by Floyd Hunter, C.
Wright Mills, Peter Bachrach and Morton S. Baratz among
others; the pluralists are represented by Robert Dahl, Nelson Polsby and others. The elitists claim that community
power structures are controlled by a relatively small clique
of decision-makers; they take note that overt action in the

decision-making process is not necessary to the operation of influence by the clique, for their reactions will be anticipated. The pluralists argue that decision-making is widely dispersed over issue areas and that when actual decisions are studied, many persons, representing all levels of society, participate in the making of decisions according to their various issue interests.

Although community power has many dimensions, e. g., anticipated reactions, legitimacy of authority, size of participant bodies, issue saliency and issue visibility, etc., it is the dimension of power stratification which is most central to the contest. The questions asked are: Is power stratified? If it is, why? If it is, how is it distributed?

Drawing any comparative generalizations about community power at this stage of the research process is definitely premature, and in most cases impossible, due to data bases which do not allow for valid comparisons; however, it appears that sound generalizations about specific political environments can be made. The dimensions of the base for community power which have been identified, e. g., money and credit, control of information sources, etc., are relatively well accepted by both sides in the argument. Power bases seem to be stratified in most cases, yet different power structures are to be found in different communities. The most important question to be answered with respect to power stratification seems to be not whether there is an operative elite, but rather, what are the conditions under which different types of power structures are likely to arise.

Lately, community power studies have begun to focus upon the need to know what the outputs of community decision-making are, and how these outputs impact the community. If one contends that knowing who the decision-makers are and how they make their decisions is sufficient to answer what the impacts are, this is a simplification of the decision-making process. What is of interest about the output focus is the distribution of benefits within the community resulting from the decisions which are made. For example, an urban renewal project may provide a new bank which creates many new jobs, but jobs largely for suburban commuters; the benefit to those who once worked or resided where the bank now stands may be only the desolation of their familiar turf, plus housing and jobs which are different but often not any better.

Researchers are now looking at more than the impacts of simple overt decisions; they also look at arenas where no decisions are made. This approach may indicate more about power structure than has previously come to light. Interest in non-decision-making is not new, but increased attention is being paid to this dimension of the dynamic. The new focus is primarily concerned with policy output, and includes not only "... who gets what and how, but who gets left out and how."[25] That this approach is less "controllable" is undoubtedly true, but it may lead to a more accurate description of the community power complex. Excellent descriptive case studies of community power structures are still necessary in order to create a base for comparative analytical studies. It is to be hoped that organizations such as the National Opinion Research Center will soon have a base of standardized data which is large enough to allow for powerful comparative studies.[26]

The concept of power is not one which applies only at the local level or only in the public sphere. Generalizations about power are expected to be applicable across all levels and sponsorship situations. Perhaps one of the ma-

jor failures inherent in community power studies is their
parochialism. The parochialism charge can be made against
power structure studies of poverty programs along a functional, i. e. , intent, instead of a territorial dimension.
When the thrust of specific poverty projects became political,
some participants and research observers expected that
there would be a reverberating redistribution of power.
However, poverty programs, regardless of funding source,
have been in almost every case dependent, often legally,
upon the consensus of the established leadership which co-
operated in their creation; therefore, power redistribution
was hardly a realistic outcome to be expected from the
minute pressure which could be exerted by the projects and
their advocates alone.

Conflicting findings by social scientists about community power structures have not reduced the reliance on
power as an important concept for the understanding of how
political systems work. Looking at power from a more cosmopolitan view may help to put the argument between power
elitists and pluralists in better perspective. Whatever the
configuration of the power structure at the local level, however, there is no doubt that there are those who have and
get, and those who have not and get not. Evidence for this
statement is provided by the figures cited in the following
paragraph.

In March of 1966, the President of the United States
directed the Secretary of the Department of Health, Education and Welfare to search for ways to improve the nation's
ability to chart its social progress. The outcome of that
directive was a publication, Toward a Social Report.
". . . Since the mid-1940's there has been little observable
change in the overall distribution of income. The lowest 20

percent of households have consistently received 5 percent
or less of personal income and less than 4 percent of total
money income. "[27] In 1966 the highest one-fifth of the population was receiving 43. 8 percent of the total money income
and the lowest three-fifths of the population was receiving
31. 6 percent of the total income.   The share of the top two-
fifths was thus 68. 4 percent. [28]   These statistical "facts"
certainly can be used to support the contention that there is
a "mobilization of bias" in this country and that there is
definitely a group which seems to receive rather an unbal-
anced share of what is available for distribution.

    Herbert Marcuse states his view of the social situa-
tion in a most convincing way:

> The mass democracy developed by monopoly capi-
> talism has shaped the rights and liberties which it
> grants in its own image and interest.   The major-
> ity of the people is the majority of their masters;
> deviations are easily 'contained'; and concentrated
> power can afford to tolerate (perhaps even defend)
> radical dissent as long as the latter complies with
> the established rules and manners (and even a little
> beyond it.)   The opposition is thus sucked in to the
> very world which it opposes--and by the very
> mechanisms which allow its development and or-
> ganization: the opposition without a mass basis is
> frustrated in its efforts to obtain such a mass
> basis.   Under these circumstances, working ac-
> cording to the rules and methods of democratic
> legality appears as surrender to the prevailing
> power structure.   And yet, it would be fatal to
> abandon the defense of civil rights and liberties
> within the established framework.   But as monopo-
> ly capitalism is compelled to extend and fortify its
> dominion at home and abroad, the democratic
> struggle will come into increasing conflict with the
> existing democratic institution with its built-in
> barriers and conservative dynamic. [29]

The Meaning of Citizen Participation

The question raised in the previous section about power, i. e., what it is, how it is used, who has it and what difference it makes to have it, are, of course, central to an understanding of the concept of citizen participation. For, if community power structures are peopled by a self-perpetuating elite which seeks to maintain its position of control over the distribution of benefits, and only occasionally allows for concessions in order to retain its legitimacy and stave off conflict, then the mobilization of low-status participatory groups whose sentiments may be antagonistic to those supporting the prevailing mobilization is self-defeating, not to mention deceitful and potentially dangerous. As Aaron Wildavsky puts it, it is a recipe for violence:

> Promise a lot; deliver a little. Lead people to believe they will be much better off, but let there be no dramatic improvement. Try a variety of small programs, each interesting but marginal in impact and severely underfinanced. Avoid any attempted solution remotely comparable in size to the dimensions of the problem you are trying to solve. Have middle-class civil servants hire upper-class student radicals to use lower-class Negroes as a battering ram against the existing local political systems; then complain that people are going around disrupting things and chastise local politicians for not cooperating with those out to do them in. Get some poor people involved in local decision-making, only to discover that there is not enough at stake to be worth bothering about. Feel guilty about what has happened to black people; tell them you are surprised they have not revolted before; express shock and dismay when they follow your advice. Go in for a little force, just enough to anger, not enough to discourage. Feel guilty again; say you are surprised that worse has not happened. Alternate with a little suppression. Mix well, apply a match, and run... 30

It is indeed difficult for social scientists to assess
the extent to which political and social institutions satisfy the
democratic values that Americans profess to hold.   It is
even more difficult to know to what extent individual autonomy
or liberty is perceived by American citizens.   Yet, Americans feel that citizen participation is a right.   Although it
appears clear that many, if not most, citizens allow the
ever-increasing political sphere to be controlled by others,
as this sphere closes off personal liberty, more and more
citizens may be aroused to participate; or perhaps these citizens may loudly refuse to participate, and undermine the
legitimacy of the representative government.   If it is true
that American society is largely undemocratic and may in
fact be systematically suppressing opportunity for certain
segments of its population, then the factors which contribute
to these situations must be identified and analyzed--as they
are, by politicians, philosophers, historians, social scientists and citizens.   Citizen participation is a vital and necessary part of American political life, both symbolically and
substantively at this time, but to impute either diabolical
or heavenly attributes to its capacity to restructure American society is unrealistic.   To study it as a process is a
necessary component in the attempt to gain a more systematic understanding of the complex system that is American
society.

Modern communications technology, increased physical mobility, and the increased knowledge of institutional
and personal behavior which is made possible by social science analysis have made not a few Americans realize that
there are indeed many discrepancies between what they value
and believe and what in actuality exists.   The knowledge of
discrepancies has often been the spark that ignites political

reform movements; yet whether the increased distribution of the knowledge of discrepancies throughout society will lead to increased political agitation is unknown. It is generally believed that lack of information leads to disengagement, but that information overload leads to a very disquieted frustration and confusion. The American public library purports to be the institution which provides informational services, in the name of societal common interest, to all citizens. However, the conventional wisdom of the field, supported by recent empirical studies of library use, [31] clearly indicates that in terms of institutional use, the public library in reality acts as a special interest institution catering to the higher levels of the socioeconomic class structure.

My encounters with the many concepts of and issues surrounding citizen participation which are discussed in this chapter, especially those bearing upon the importance of equality of access to information in a democratic society, served as the foundation from which to explore research needs in the area of citizen participation. The encounters, coupled with an interest in the American public library as a public service institution, initiated the specific project which is reported in the chapters which follow.

The project's concern is confined to the American public library and makes no attempt to relate or link this institution's experiences with citizen participation to the experiences of other service institutions; nor does the study deal with the larger question of the role of the public library as an information source and/or service for all persons as they attempt to maintain or create a democratic society in America.

Notes

1. For an explication of the difference between life-style
    and system-maintenance functions see Oliver P. Wil-
    liams, "Life Style Values and Political Decentraliza-
    tion in Metropolitan Areas, " Southwestern Social Sci-
    ence Quarterly, XLVIII (December, 1967), pp. 299-
    310. Also, for an interesting report of research
    along similar lines see Charles S. Benson and Peter
    B. Lund, Neighborhood Distribution of Local Public
    Services (Berkeley: University of California, Insti-
    tute of Governmental Studies, 1969).

2. This phenomenon has, of course, been recognized pre-
    viously in other "ideological" subcultures within so-
    ciety such as the beatniks of the 1950's.

3. Edmund M. Burke, "Citizen Participation Strategies, "
    Journal of the American Institute of Planners, XXXIV
    (September, 1968), p. 287.

4. Murray Edelman, The Symbolic Uses of Politics (Ur-
    bana: University of Illinois Press, 1967), pp. 188-
    194.

5. At this juncture, it is well to remember Charles Lind-
    blom's warning that with respect to controversial pro-
    grams, when the purpose is made clear, quite often
    the "jig is up. " This is certainly supported by many
    studies of the Community Action programs, notably
    Ralph M. Kramer, Participation of the Poor (Engle-
    wood Cliffs, N.J.: Prentice-Hall, 1969); Kenneth
    Clark and Jeannette Hopkins, A Relevant War Against
    Poverty (New York: Harper, 1970); and Brandeis
    University. Florence Heller School for Advanced
    Studies in Social Welfare, Community Representation
    in Community Action Programs; Final Report (Spring-
    field, Va.: Clearinghouse for Federal Scientific and
    Technical Information, March 1969), PB 108 013.
    In these studies, projects which concentrated upon
    developing or utilizing effective, penetrating decision-
    making by other than the traditional authority struc-
    ture were met with high levels of animosity, and in
    almost every case were restructured or discontinued.
    This was true regardless of the intent behind the de-
    velopment of the effective decision-making power.
    The usual intents were either to attack the psycho-

logical problem of inefficacy feelings, or to socialize
the poor into political life; their intent, only rarely,
was to challenge the legitimacy of the existing power
structure.

6.   Jack Rothman, "An Analysis of Goals and Roles in
     Community Organization Practice, " Social Work, IX
     (April, 1964), pp. 24-25.

7.   Paul E. Peterson, "Forms of Representation: Partici-
     pation of the Poor in the Community Action Program, "
     American Political Science Review, LXIV (June, 1970),
     pp. 491-492.

8.   Ibid., pp. 491-507, for example.

9.   Burke, op. cit. Burke suggests that although citizen
     participation is often predicted upon value premises,
     it is more often a strategy due mostly to practical
     considerations. He sees five citizen participation
     strategies: education-therapy, behavioral change,
     staff supplement, cooptation and community power.

10. Hans B. C. Spiegel and Stephen D. Mittenthal, "The
     Many Faces of Citizen Participation: A Bibliographic
     Overview, " Citizen Participation in Urban Develop-
     ment, Vol. I.: Concepts and Issues, ed. Hans B. C.
     Spiegel (Washington, D.C.: NTL Institute for Applied
     Behavioral Science, 1968), p. 3.

11. Kramer, loc. cit.

12. Michael Lipsky, "Protest as a Political Resource, "
     American Political Science Review, LXII (September,
     1968), pp. 1144-1158.

13. Richard A. Cloward, "Are the Poor Left Out?" The
     Nation, CCI (August 2, 1965), p. 55.

14. E. E. Schattschneider, The SemiSovereign People (New
     York: Holt, Rinehart and Winston, 1960). Schatt-
     schneider contends on the basis of empirical evidence
     that the political pressure system "is skewed, loaded
     and unbalanced in favor of a fraction of a minority
     [i.e., the upper socio-economic classes]" (p. 35).
     For a full discussion of the concept see especially
     pp. 20-46.

15. Edward C. Banfield, The Unheavenly City (Boston:
     Little, Brown, 1970), p. 211.

16. James Q. Wilson, "Planning and Politics: Citizen Par-
     ticipation in Urban Renewal, " Journal of the American
     Institute of Planners, XXIX (November, 1963), p. 245.

17. Views that support the contention that applying the con-
     cept of culture to the life-style patterns in lower-
     class society is a misapplication can be found in
     works such as: Kenneth Clark, Dark Ghetto (New
     York: Harper, 1965); Herbert Gans, The Urban Vil-
     lagers (New York: Macmillan, 1962); Hylan Lewis,
     "Culture, Class and Family Life Among Low-Income
     Urban Negroes, " Arthur M. Ross and Herbert Hill
     (eds.), Employment, Race, and Poverty (New York:
     Harcourt, Brace and World, 1967); and, Charles A.
     Valentine, Culture and Poverty (Chicago: University
     of Chicago Press, 1968).

18. Works supportive of the culture of poverty view are
     those such as: Oscar Lewis, Five Families (New
     York: Basic Books, 1959); David Matza, "The Dis-
     reputable Poor"; Neil J. Smelser and Seymour M.
     Lipset (eds.), Social Structure and Mobility in Eco-
     nomic Development (Chicago: Aldine, 1966); and,
     Daniel P. Moyniham, The Negro Family (Washington,
     D. C.: Government Printing Office, 1965).

19. Elliot Liebow, Tally's Corner (Boston: Little, Brown,
     1967), p. 209.

20. Ibid. , p. 223.

21. S. M. Miller and Martin Rein, "Participation, Poverty
     and Administration, " Public Administration Review,
     XXIX (January-February, 1969), p. 17.

22. Milton Rokeach and Seymour Parker, "Values as Social
     Indicators of Poverty and Race Relations in Ameri-
     ca, " Annals of the American Academy of Political
     and Social Sciences, no. 388 (April, 1970), p. 103,
     106.

23. Michael Lipsky, "Toward a Theory of Street-Level
     Bureaucracy. " Paper prepared for presentation at
     the Annual Meeting of the American Political Science

Association, New York, September 2-6, 1969.

24.   Two excellent articles dealing with such methodological
      aspects as reputational technique, decision sociometry
      and non-decision identification are: L. Vaughn Blank-
      enship, "Community Power and Decision-making: A
      Comparative Evaluation of Measurement Techniques, "
      Social Forces, XLIII (October, 1964), p. 207-16; and,
      Richard M. Merelman, "On the Neo-Elitist Critique
      of Community Power, " American Political Science Re-
      view, LXII (June, 1968), pp. 451-60.   A bibliography
      of methodological studies is: Walter E. Clark,
      Community Power and Decision-Making (Monticello,
      Ill.:   Council of Planning Librarians, November
      1971.)   Exchange Bibliography no. 234.

25.   Peter Bachrach and Morton S. Baratz, Power and Pov-
      erty; Theory and Practice (New York: Oxford Univer-
      sity Press, 1970), p. 105.

26.   Behavior Today, III (January 17, 1972) announced that
      NORC has devised a preliminary questionnaire that
      provides for the gathering of "all purpose sociologi-
      cal data. "

27.   U.S. Department of Health, Education and Welfare,
      Toward A Social Report (Washington, D.C.:   Govern-
      ment Printing Office, 1969), p. 42.

28.   Ibid., p. 44.

29.   Herbert Marcuse, An Essay on Liberation (Boston:
      Beacon Press, 1969), pp. 64-65.

30.   Moynihan, Maximum Feasible Misunderstanding, op. cit.,
      verso of title page.

31.   Many of these studies are cited throughout the remain-
      ing chapters of this study.

Chapter 2

SURVEY DATA ANALYSES

In analyzing the data there are three principal concerns. The first is to describe the policy making style,
citizen participation pattern and service goal priorities in
public libraries in order to discover commonalities and dis-
similarities. An investigation of library literature prior to
the initiation of the study uncovered little systematic investigation of the above characteristics. [1] It is the author's belief that knowledge of these factors may provide helpful clues
in the quest for more effective library services. The
second concern is to investigate whether a decentralized policy making style is found in association with an active citizen participation pattern and, further, to see if libraries
with an active citizen participation pattern tend to view their
service goal priorities differently from libraries with an inactive citizen participation pattern. The assumption under-
lying a possible association between decentralized policy
making and active citizen participation was drawn from research findings in industrial sociology and organization
theory. [2] The assumption was made that the models of effective decision-making in industrial and other formal organizations might also have value in service organizations.
This assumption is also supported by research findings. [3]
As to the effect citizen participation has on library service

goals, it is assumed that a new source of input into the decision-making process might well be expected to alter outputs.   Chapter 4 discusses in detail the foundations for this
assumption and, further, indicates why the direction of that
change could be expected to be in the direction of increased
information-orientation of services.   The third concern here
is to provide the basis from which illustrative case study
sites could be drawn.

Policy Making Style

This section attempts to discover the degree to which
the resources of the libraries surveyed are centralized or
decentralized in terms of buildings, collections and utilization of professional employees.   In addition an analysis of
how each respondent perceives the direction of decision-
making flow for policy matters at his library is presented.
Further, the extent to which various participant groups take
an active role in decision arenas is discussed in relation to
the dimension of centralization/decentralization.

a.   Physical Decentralization

Table 1 indicates one measure of the degree to which
the public library is a physically decentralized community
service.   The mean number of branches for the responding
libraries is 2. 7.   Of the 102 libraries with branches that
responded, the average number of branches is 9. 9.

Some of the libraries which responded (14) were library system headquarters.   Respondents in this category
were instructed to consider member libraries as branches.
A sub-analysis of these 14 libraries revealed no significant

TABLE 1:   NUMBER OF BRANCHES

Stratum	No. of Branches	Total No. of Libraries in Stratum	Total No. of Branches in Stratum
1	0-	28	0
2	1- 2	27	41
3	3- 8	37	182
4	9-24	29	358
5	25- +	11	447
		132	1028

differences between system headquarters and central libraries
with regard to decision-making structure and library goals.
A major difference, as would be expected, was found in response to the question concerning branch library boards.
Many system libraries maintain independent library boards.
At this stage of the development of library systems, many
members remain quite autonomous; therefore, it was decided
to remove these 14 libraries from the analysis of branch library advisory boards.   (See the section below on Citizen
Participation Pattern).   Although answers from library systems affected other questions, e.g., the ratio of professional
employees working inside the central facility to those working outside, it was felt that the inclusion of the system responses would not significantly affect the analyses; therefore,
they are included in all other question analyses.

       In further analyzing the physical decentralization of
the libraries, data for bookmobiles and for deposit stations
were grouped into categories for the purpose of analysis.
Seventy-one (71) percent of the responding libraries indicated
that they had bookmobile service.   Table 2 outlines the percentage distribution of number of bookmobile stops.   As
can be seen in Table 2, 44 percent of the libraries have
between 20 and 99 bookmobile stops; further, 57 percent

TABLE 2: PERCENTAGE DISTRIBUTION
OF BOOKMOBILE STOPS

Category Code	No. of Stops in Category	No. of Libraries	Percent in Category
1	none	39	29. 5%
2	1- 19	18	13. 6
3	20- 49	38	28. 8
4	50- 99	20	15. 2
5	100-199	13	9. 8
6	200- +	4	3. 1
		132	100. 0%

of the libraries have 20 or more stops.

The same type of data for deposit stations is given in Table 3.

TABLE 3: PERCENTAGE DISTRIBUTION
OF DEPOSIT STATIONS

Category Code	No. of Stations in Category	No. of Libraries	Percent in Category
1	none	79	59. 9%
2	1-10	36	27. 3
3	11-25	11	8. 3
4	26- +	6	4. 5
		132	100. 0%

Although not as many libraries have deposit stations as bookmobile service, 40 percent do have at least one deposit station.   Thus, based upon these three measures of physical
resources, these libraries are quite decentralized.

b.   Administrative Decentralization

As a measure of administrative decentralization respondents were asked, for both bookmobile service and de-

posit stations, if these services were administered directly
from one or more branch libraries. The analysis shows
that both services are highly controlled by the central administration: of the 93 libraries with bookmobile service 81
(87%) indicated that administrative authority was centralized;
of the 53 libraries with deposit stations, 43 (81%) administered them from the central facility.

With regard to the utilization of professional staff outside the main library building, once again the data were
grouped for analysis purposes. Table 4 shows the distribution.

TABLE 4:   PERCENT OF PROFESSIONAL EMPLOYEES
WORKING OUTSIDE OF MAIN LIBRARY

Category	% of Professionals Working Outside Main Library	No. of Libraries	% in Category
1	0-19%	41	39.8%
2	20-39%	34	33.1
3	40-59%	19	18.4
4	60-79%	6	5.8
5	80- +	3	2.9
		103	100.0%

When devising the code for this question it was felt
that even though a library did not have branch facilities,
there was no reason why some librarians might not have as-
signment outside of the central facility. For example, if
the library had several deposit stations, one staff member
might spend the majority of his time visiting these stations;
or, a library that was a member of a system, though not
its headquarters, might assign a staff member to some system function outside of the library building; or, a librarian
might be assigned as a liaison between some other community

institution and the library. Responses to this question indicate that professional positions in the responding libraries without branches are literally in these libraries. None of the libraries without branches which responded indicated any professionals assigned outside of the main library building.

As Table 4 indicates, professional positions are highly centralized. The Table excludes the 28 libraries without branches which responded to the survey. It shows that 40 percent of all libraries with branches have less than 20 percent of their professionals working outside of the central library. Had the 28 libraries without branches been included in the analysis, the Table would have shown that over half (52 percent) of the libraries have less than 20 percent of their professionals working outside the main library. Looking at the data from another point of view, only nine of the libraries with branches reported having 60 percent or more of their professionals working outside the main library; all had at least 23 branches.

c. Decision-making Style

In an attempt to capture a capsule view of the direction of decision-making flow in the libraries, each respondent was asked to choose that one of four diagrams presented (see the questionnaire, item 6, in Appendix B) which best illustrates policy decision-making at his library. No words were used to describe the diagrams on the questionnaire. The diagrams were drawn to express the following management system as conceptualized by Rensis Likert: A, exploitive authoritative; B, benevolent authoritative; C, consultative; and D, participative.[4] I prefer a less judgmental choice of words to describe the diagrams. The decision-

making styles thus become: A, authoritative; B, cooperative; C, integrative; and D, participative. These decision-
making styles can be conceptualized as a continuum ranging
from authoritative to participative as given below:

Authoritative	Cooperative	Integrative	Participative

Diagram A, authoritative, is quite direct; the final
decision goes out from a central source, or from the top of
the hierarchy. The cooperative diagram, (B), is considered
to be restrictive in nature because even though it provides
for feedback, it does not allow for discussion or group activity on the part of the subordinate units; each unit deals
directly with the superior unit, but without the support of
other similar units. Diagram C, integrative, is also basically restrictive because feedback is limited; it is, however,
further towards the participative end of the continuum because it allows for communication among subordinates. [One
might also view this type of flow as subversive--the subordinates girding up for an assault on the superior.] The participative diagram (D), is straightforward; the decision-making flow allows all units to be in communication with one
another, and hierarchy plays a limited role.

Table 5 demonstrates the librarians' view of decision-
making flow at their respective libraries. The more restrictive end of the continuum contains 71 percent of the
cases.

It could be argued that librarians who responded by
marking the cooperative diagram (B), really believe that the
decision-making style at their libraries is basically participative, and had respondents been given written definitions to
go along with the diagrams, a significant number of them

TABLE 5:   DIRECTION OF DECISION-MAKING FLOW
FOR MAJOR POLICY DECISIONS

Decision style category	Frequency	Percent
Authoritative	31	25. 2%
Cooperative	52	42. 3
Integrative	4	3. 2
Participative	36	29. 3
	123	100. 0%

would have chosen diagram D instead of B.   In response to
this argument: 1) the participative diagram was as available as the cooperative one and could easily have been chos-
en providing one assumes that all the diagrams were perused
before a choice was made; 2) respondents in the validity and
reliability analyses and in the response bias study chose the
same proportion of each diagram; and 3) if a respondent did
choose the first diagram that he saw which appeared to him
to reflect a participative style, it seems fair to say that the
diagrams correctly reflect decision-making flow in various
restrictive degrees; therefore, it is the respondent's perception of what constitutes participative decision-making that
is out of perspective.

One respondent made this point quite candidly.   He
circled diagram D, participative, but then asterisked his
answer and drew the following diagram with the note, "As
seen by administrative assistant":

d.   Participants

Four items on the questionnaire attempt to elicit the degree to which various groups participate in decision-making affecting policy for the library.   Two questions, 7 and 8, called for the respondents' perceptions of the extent to which professional and non-professional staff are involved in the policy making process.   Table 6 details the difference in participation between professional and non-professional employees.

TABLE 6:   EXTENT OF PROFESSIONAL AND NON-
PROFESSIONAL INVOLVEMENT IN POLICY MAKING PROCESS

Category	Professionals		Non-Professionals	
	Frequency	%	Frequency	%
Fully involved	72	54. 5%	12	9. 1%
Often consulted, but not ordinarily involved in the actual process	53	40. 2	77	58. 3
Occasionally consulted, but rarely involved in the actual process	7	5. 3	42	31. 8
Never involved	0	0. 0	1	. 8
	132	100. 0%	132	100. 0%

The results are as expected.   Professionals are fully involved in over 50 percent of the libraries while non-professionals are fully involved in only 9 percent.   The results add further credence to the view that libraries adhere to a centralized or authoritative decision-making style, as almost half (46 percent) the respondents indicated that the professional staff was either not ordinarily or rarely involved in actual decisions.   For non-professional staff, 91 percent were not ordinarily, rarely or never involved in the actual decision-making process.

In order to get a more precise picture of policy making in libraries, a decision-making matrix was provided in
which respondents were to indicate, in ten specific decision
areas, which of seven participant groups played an <u>active</u>
role. The decision-making areas listed are: 1) <u>Personnel</u>:
(a) selection of head librarian; (b) selection of professionals;
(c) selection of non-professionals; (d) salary; and, (e) promotions; 2) <u>Budget Preparation</u>; 3) <u>Materials Selection</u>;
4) <u>Program Determination</u>; and 5) Facilities: (a) building design; and (b) site selection. The categories of participants
are: 1) Library board; 2) Head librarian; 3) Key administrative staff; 4) Professionals; 5) Non-professionals; 6) Citizen groups; and 7) Others (which includes governing authori-
ties, specialists, labor unions, etc.).

The total results for all libraries by each of the five
main decision-making areas are given in Figures IA and IB;
total results for all decision areas are given in Figure II.
A comparison between Figure II and Table 6 for the categories of professional and non-professional staff participation
indicates that the responses to the more general questions
on participation (questions 7 and 8) give a valid impression
of the decision-making style.

CATEGORY	TABLE 6	FIGURE II
Professionals fully involved	54. 5%	54. 0%
Non-professionals fully involved	9. 1	6. 0

If one then also considers the results from Table 5, in
which 71 percent of the respondents were categorized towards
the more restrictive half of the decision-making style continuum, the total picture indicates that libraries tend to make
(cont. on p. 41)

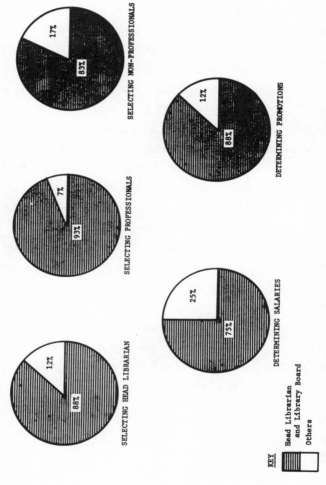

FIGURE IA: PERCENT OF PARTICIPATION BY PARTICIPANT CATEGORIES
FOR ALL RESPONDING LIBRARIES: DECISIONS EFFECTING PERSONNEL*

SELECTING NON-PROFESSIONALS

17%

83%

DETERMINING PROMOTIONS

12%

88%

SELECTING PROFESSIONALS

7%

93%

SELECTING HEAD LIBRARIAN

12%

88%

DETERMINING SALARIES

25%

75%

KEY

Head Librarian
and Library Board

Others

*See questionnaire item number 9, Appendix A. This Figure represents the average total participation for
all responding libraries in the decision-making area cited.

FIGURE IB: PERCENT OF PARTICIPATION BY PARTICIPANT CATEGORIES FOR ALL RESPONDING LIBRARIES:
DECISIONS EFFECTING BUDGET, MATERIALS, PROGRAMS AND FACILITIES*

PROGRAM PLANNING

28%
19%
53%

SITE SELECTION

9%
8%
83%

MATERIALS SELECTION

7%
23%
70%

BUILDING DESIGN

7%
20%
73%

BUDGET PREPARATION

2%
14%
84%

KEY

Head Librarian and
Library Board

Citizens

Others

*See questionnaire item number 9, Appendix A. This Figure represents the average total participation for
all responding libraries in the decision-making area cited.

FIGURE II: PERCENT OF PARTICIPATION BY PARTICIPANT
CATEGORIES FOR ALL RESPONDING LIBRARIES: ACROSS
ALL DECISION-MAKING AREAS*

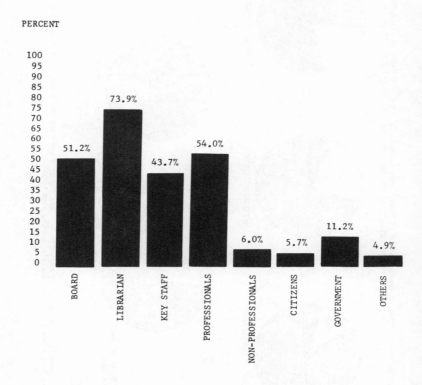

*See questionnaire item number 9, Appendix B.   The Figure
represents the average total participation for all responding
libraries for all decision-making areas.

policy at the highest administrative level. There is limited
participation by non-administrative professional staff and
from subordinate physical units; also, there is minimal participation by non-professional staff.

An analysis of the 36 libraries which reported their
decision-making style for policy matters as participative was
undertaken in order to determine whether there was a group
of "participative" libraries. The analysis showed that all
these libraries rated their professionals as fully involved
and their non-professionals as either fully involved or often
consulted. Of the twelve (12) libraries which stated that
their non-professional staff was fully involved, all indicated
they had a participative decision-making style. As a group,
the 36 libraries tended to include more categories of participants in each of the specific decision-making areas. This
is particularly evident with regard to the categories: selection of professional staff, selection of non-professional staff
and determination of library programs. However, these libraries were not strikingly alike or different from the other
libraries with respect to their citizen participation pattern
or library service orientation; still, 1) they accounted for
the major portion of favorable attitudes towards citizen participation (15 of the 34 libraries were classified as receptive); and 2) they constituted the major portion (5 of 9 cases)
of those libraries exhibiting the most active citizen participation pattern.

e.   Summary

In order to create a measure for policy-making style
which would allow for classification of each library on a
single continuum, a scale made up from a number of ques-

42   Citizen Participation

tionnaire items was constructed.   The continuum was divided
into six categories.   These categories are listed below in
Table 7, which gives the frequency and percent of libraries
in each category.   As can easily be seen, once again the
more centralized, authoritative or restrictive half of the continuum contains the majority of the cases, 65 percent or 86
of the 132 cases.

TABLE 7:   POLICY MAKING STYLE

Category	Frequency	Percent
Highly Centralized	5	3.8%
Centralized	46	34.7
Moderately Centralized	35	26.5
Moderately Decentralized	41	31.1
Decentralized	4	3.1
Highly Decentralized	1	.8
	132	100.0%

Citizen Participation Pattern

Citizen participation in this analysis is limited to
participation by organized groups of citizens; it does not re-
fer to actions taken by individuals.   It is assumed that at
least the majority of libraries have some means by which
individuals can make recommendations for materials or services, e.g., suggestion boxes.   Of course, citizen participation in the form of library boards has and continues to be
a major source of potential input for public library policy
making.   In 1968 there were some 61,000 public library
trustees associated with the vast majority of the 6,922 public libraries.[5]

a. Library Boards

During the past four decades, there have been a substantial number of widely read studies on library boards, [6]
not to mention the several hundred commentaries available.
On the basis of these studies it has become somewhat conventional wisdom that board members tend to be: 1) older;
2) descriptively representative of only a small segment of
the community populace; 3) of minor political importance in
the community; and 4) that once they are appointed, or less
frequently elected, they tend to hold on to their positions
doggedly. [7]

The main concern of this study is on the participation
of citizens outside of the legitimate or traditional forms of
the library board and the Friends of the Library; however,
a brief, focused look at these two groups was taken in order
to provide a more complete picture of citizen participation.
In regard to library boards, information on the following
characteristics was sought: 1) the extent to which the form
exists; 2) whether board members are predominately appointed or elected; 3) descriptive characteristics of members; and 4) the role of the board in policy making.

Predominance of library board form. The library
board remains a predominant organizational form on the
American public library scene. Of the 132 responding libraries, 122 (92 percent) reported that they had some type
of library board associated with the library. In the re-
maining ten libraries without boards, the library was reported as being directly responsible to either a city or
county governing authority.

Way in which the boards are constituted. Appointment is the predominant means by which board members win

their seats. Eighty-eight percent of the responding libraries
reported that their members were primarily appointed, while
only 8 percent indicated that their members were elected.
Of the 21 libraries which reported some "other" method of
board constitution, in 16 cases they are primarily appoint-
ments by a wide variety of officials; e. g., "2 appointed by
school board, 1 by library board; 3 by city council and 1 by
mayor. " Five of the "other" cases showed that a majority
of the board members are elected. Table 8 illustrates the
results of the responses.

    In terms of a strictly formalistic view of representa-
tion, i. e., by looking at representation solely in terms of
the arrangements which establish the way in which a representative is selected, [8] library boards tend to represent city
and /or county chief executives and councils rather than the
citizens of these governmental units. Using directness of
selection as the criterion for formal representation, constituents are very indirectly represented by library board members. In only five cases in this study are library board
members directly representative of the populace, i. e., they
are elected at large. In four cases board members were
directly representative of persons residing in special districts, e. g., wards or school districts. In five additional
cases, at least one board member was elected at large or
elected from a special district.

    Descriptive representation. An attempt was made to
make a rough assessment of the degree to which library
board members were representative of their constituents in
terms of socially descriptive representation. Socially descriptive representation refers to such characteristics as the
social class, ethnic or racial background, age, and place of
residence of the representatives themselves. [9] Three char-

TABLE 8:   METHOD OF LIBRARY BOARD CONSTITUTION

Method	Frequency	Percent
Appointed primarily by a private library group	9	7. 5%
Appointed primarily by city/county chief executive	20	16. 7
Appointed primarily by city/county council	61	50. 8
Elected from school district	1	. 8
Elected from electoral district	3	2. 5
Elected at large	5	4. 2
Other	21	17. 5
	120	100. 0%

acteristics of board members were used in the analysis of socially descriptive representation: 1) occupation (dichotomized into predominantly white collar and other); 2) race; and 3) age (to the nearest decade).   These three characteristics were then investigated in association with the following three 1960 Census characteristics of that governmental unit which was most closely representative of the library's service area: 1) percent white collar employees;[10] 2) percent black;[11] and 3) median age. [12]

Occupation: Table 9 gives frequencies and percents of white collar employees in the library service areas.

TABLE 9:   PERCENT WHITE COLLAR EMPLOYEES
IN SERVICE AREAS

Percent White Collar	Number of Libraries	Percent of Libraries
0-34%	34	29. 0%
35-44	40	34. 2
45-54	31	26. 5
55-64	9	7. 7
65- +	3	2. 6
	117	100. 0%

Table 10 below incorporates the findings in Table 9
with the results of a classification of the library boards into
a traditional/non-traditional dichotomy. The classification
of a board as non-traditional was made as inclusive and non-
restrictive as possible. Students, clerical and sales personnel and farmers, as well as blue collar employees such
as shop foremen and other types of lower-level supervisory
personnel were included in the non-traditional category; in
other words, any person who was not clearly of a profes-
sional/managerial occupational type and was not a housewife
was considered a non-traditional board member. [13] Even
with this loose definition, only 11 of these 117 boards had
at least one member from the non-traditional category. The
boards are thus overwhelmingly (91 percent) dominated by
traditional board members. In only 9 percent of the cases
was at least one member of the library board classified as
of the non-traditional type. Table 10 below demonstrates
the percent of libraries and the percent of library boards
with at least one non-traditional board member according to
a five-part categorization of service areas by the percent of

TABLE 10:   PERCENT OF LIBRARIES AND PERCENT OF
LIBRARIES WITH BOARDS HAVING AT LEAST ONE NON-
TRADITIONAL BOARD MEMBER, BY SERVICE AREA
CONSTITUENCY

Percent of Service Area Constituency Categorized as Non-White Collar	Percent of Surveyed Libraries in Service Area Categories	Percent of Surveyed Libraries with at Least one Non-tradi- tional Board Member
100-66%	29. 0%	. 0%
65-56	34. 2	1. 7
55-46	26. 5	5. 1
45-36	7. 7	2. 6
35-0	2. 6	. 0
	100. 0%	9. 4%

the constituency classified as non-white collar. Clearly,
these library boards are not representative of their service
area constituencies in terms of an occupational dichotomy.
It appears, though, that when the occupational mix is more
nearly even, i. e., a service area is neither predominantly
white collar or non-white collar, a library is more likely
to have at least one non-traditional board member; however,
non-traditional board members remain rare regardless of
the occupational mix of the constituency area.

 Race: It is important to make clear at the outset of
this section that no subtle, or even not so subtle, condem-
nation is implied by the findings of the racial composition of
the boards. In fact, no negative implication is forwarded
for any of the socially descriptive data. Race is included
as a traditional measure of socially descriptive representation (as are occupation and age of representatives) and because it does serve to underline what librarians have known
for a long time, which is simply that not many library
board members are black.[14] The findings presented here
merely indicate that the situation has not changed much and
that in terms of representing their service area constituencies (not service area users necessarily) library boards
are not representative in terms of their racial composition.

 Table 11 details the frequency of cases by percent
black on the library board. Due to the rather small size
of many of the library boards the percent figures must be
interpreted accordingly;[15] however, it is felt that the table
as constructed gives a useful indication of the racial composition of the boards.

 Table 12 contrasts percent black on library boards
with percent black in the libraries service areas.

TABLE 11:   PERCENT BLACK ON LIBRARY BOARDS

Percent Category	Frequency	Percent
None	73	65. 8%
Less than 20	27	25. 1
20-39	9	8. 2
40 or more	1	. 9
	110	100. 0%

TABLE 12:   PERCENT BLACK ON LIBRARY BOARDS
AND IN SERVICE AREAS

On Library Boards			In Service Areas		
None	65. 8	(73)	None	13. 6	(15)
Less than 20%	25. 1	(27)	1-10%	46. 8	(51)
20 to 39%	8. 2	(9)	11-39%	33. 3	(37)
40% or more	. 9	(1)	40% or more	6. 3	(7)
TOTAL	100. 0%	(110)		100. 0%	(110)

Although only 14 percent of the library service areas contained less than one percent black population, 66 percent of
the library boards had no black members.   In only one case
were blacks apparently represented by more than their proportion in the service area population.

The occupations of the black board members were
scanned.   Except for one, a labor union official, all the
black board members were employed in traditional occupations for library board members; their occupations included
clergyman, physician, lawyer, funeral home owner, housewife, etc.

Age: Table 13, Median Age on Library Board and
in Service Area, is straightforward and needs little interpretation.   Despite the discrepancies between the collection
methods and size of data bases, this table indicates that
board members are rather older than the majority of their

service area populaces.

TABLE 13:   MEDIAN AGE ON LIBRARY BOARDS
            AND IN SERVICE AREAS

Age Categories	Percent on Library Board by Age Categories		Percent in Service Areas by Age Categories	
Less than 20	.0%	(0)	1.7%	(2)
20 - 29	.0	(0)	48.7	(58)
30 - 39	.8	(1)	47.1	(56)
40 - +	99.2	(118)	2.5	(3)
TOTAL	100.0%	(119)	100.0%	(119)

As a final gross indicator of socially descriptive representation, the sex of the library board members was obtained.   It is a well known statistic that slightly over half
of the adult. population of this country is female; however,
board members of these libraries tend to be male.   Sex was
reported for 890 board members.   Six hundred-seventy-two
(672), or 76 percent of the board members, are male; and
73 percent, 85 of the 117 boards reporting, are predominantly male.

Summary of socially descriptive criteria: The degree
to which it is important, in terms of institutional impact or
even simple use, for a public service agency to have persons in its decision-making positions who are socially descriptive of its users and/or potential users has and continues to be a subject of great debate.   (See the Preface
and Chapter I of this study for a discussion of the principal
actors and factors in this debate.)   It is obvious from the
data collected that in terms of the three criteria studied, library boards are not socially descriptive of their service
area constituencies; however, they may well be quite socially

descriptive of their user populations.

   Role in policy making. Figure II illustrated that, collectively, library boards are actively involved in all the tested decision-making areas slightly over 51 percent of the time. Their most vital role in the 122 libraries surveyed is the selection of the head librarian; in 66 percent of the cases the library board was the sole participant group reported as actively involved. (In only one case were citizen groups reported as being actively involved.) Another 22 percent of the cases reported that the library board, in conjunction with other participant groups, was actively involved in choosing the head librarian; it is difficult to determine which of the several named groups played the predominant role, but it undoubtedly is safe to assume that library boards play a predominant role in selecting the head librarian in well over 75 percent of the libraries. In combination with other groups, boards were reported as actively involved in all but 16 (12 percent) of the libraries.

TABLE 14: EXTENT OF LIBRARY BOARD INVOLVEMENT
     IN DECISION-MAKING AREAS

Decision Arena	Case Frequency	Total Cases	Percent
Selecting head librarian	116	122	95.1%
Selecting professional staff	34	120	28.3
Selecting non-professional staff	15	121	12.4
Determining salaries	85	121	70.2
Determining promotions	42	117	35.9
Budget Preparation	82	122	67.2
Materials selection	8	122	6.6
Program planning	46	121	38.0
Facilities:			
Design	92	115	80.0
Site Selection	85	109	77.9
Across all arenas: (% average)		122	51.2%

In the other decision-making arenas investigated, the board was reported as actively involved to the following extent:

Summary. There seems to be little doubt that library boards play a large role in many aspects of the public library's operations. Throughout the history of the American public library, the library board has functioned as the means by which some citizens could participate in library decision-making.[16] Although there have been major changes in the public library in terms of 1) diversity of services offered; 2) growth of the number of libraries; and 3) characteristics of large groups of potential users residing in close proximity to libraries, there has been little change in library boards, either in terms of who serves or in what decision areas they participate.

b.   Friends of the Library

Another means by which citizens have traditionally participated in library affairs is through membership in a Friends of the Library group. (A Friends group is usually organized when the library finds itself in need of extra funds, increased publicity, or subtle pressures in regard to referendum or bond issues.) One-hundred-thirty libraries responded to the question on the Friends of the Library. Fifty-eight (45 percent) of the libraries reported having Friends of the Library groups, but 16 of the 58 stated that the Friends were presently inactive; therefore, only 32 percent of the libraries had functioning Friends of the Library groups.

Although respondents were asked to give the same type of descriptive information about the leaders of the

Friends of the Library as they had about library board members, very few did; thus, no really strong evidence on the characteristics of the Friends can be given. For the 13 cases which reported data, the leaders of the Friends were quite similar to library board members in terms of occupation, race and age.

    c. Groups Attempting to Influence Library Policy

Respondents were asked to identify the kinds of citizen groups (outside of the library board, Friends of the Library, or other groups whose major orientation might be toward the library) which had attempted to influence either library policy or administrative decisions during the past year. Table 15 illustrates the responses given to this question:

TABLE 15:   GROUPS ATTEMPTING TO INFLUENCE
LIBRARY POLICY

Type of Group	Frequency
Neighborhood organization or Block Club	11
Educational	5
Religious	2
Political	2
Racial	1
	21 (19 percent of 130 respondents)

Four of the libraries reported more than one group trying to exert pressure, but only two libraries mentioned more than one type of group. In both cases where more than one type of group was mentioned, one was a neighborhood group. The libraries in this sample thus appear to receive few pressures from outside groups to influence library operations.

Although no data were collected on the kinds of demands that the above groups made, in response to a question on what kinds of library services had been suggested by citizen groups which the respondent felt the library should not offer, the following list resulted:

TABLE 16:   TYPES OF LIBRARY SERVICES REQUESTED
BY CITIZENS BUT WHICH THE LIBRARY SHOULD NOT OFFER

Type of Service	Frequency
Discussion groups	1
Local history collection	1
Referral services	3
New branch library	5
Additional deposit stations	2
Shut-in service	3
Additional audio-visual materials	5
Extended hours	6
Special collections; e.g., musical scores, dress patterns, puzzles	4

In a recent study of public library administrators and their environments, data bearing on this area of concern were also collected. The authors of this study conclude that:

> The evidence of this survey corroborates the widely shared intelligence that the particular pressures upon public libraries are modest. Where there are demands they tend to be for new branch sites and for traditional services. Specific requests for specialized services and for programs oriented to meet commitments to new and potential client groups are isolated and uncommon. The sentiment of most of the public library's public tends toward apathy and disinterest. No major interest group appears to be either consistently supportive or violently opposed. [17]

The evidence from my survey corroborates the conclusions of Drs. Bundy and Wasserman.

d.   Opportunities Created for Citizen Participation

Because attempts to influence library operations by citizen groups appear to be rather limited, it is interesting to note just what avenues are open to citizen groups through which they may exert influence. The libraries were asked to indicate whether opportunities for citizen participation in library policy making had been created, and further to briefly identify these opportunities. Respondents were given four categories of possible programs through which citizens might participate as an aid in responding. These categories were: 1) through the Model Cities Program; 2) through Office of Economic Opportunity programs; 3) through other non-library initiated programs; and 4) through library initiated programs.

TABLE 17:   OPPORTUNITIES CREATED FOR CITIZEN PARTICIPATION

Type of Program	Frequency
Model Cities	6
Office of Economic Opportunity	12
Other Non-Library Initiated Programs	1
Library Initiated Programs	17
	36 (28 percent of 128 responding libraries)

Of the 17 libraries which had initiated special programs of their own, ten had created special purpose library committees and seven had enlisted the interest of an existing com-

munity group; e. g., a drug clinic board and a block club.
Thirteen of the 36 libraries reported that there was more
than one type of program through which citizens could participate; e. g., six of these 13 libraries reported all four
types of programs as currently available opportunities through
which citizens could participate.

Although the number of libraries which reported data
for attempts to influence library operations (21) and for opportunities created for citizen participation (36) is small, it
seemed of interest to look at these two groups of libraries
in an attempt to determine whether there was any obvious relationship between having channels for participation open and
the use thereof.   Of the 21 libraries reporting attempts to
influence library operations from outside groups, ten did not
have formal channels open for citizen participation; but, of
the 36 libraries which did have formal channels open, 21 reported no attempts to influence library operations.   Although
it is difficult to interpret the responses due to the lack of
detail provided, it appears that there is simply little interest
in pressuring the library in any manner, regardless of whether there are avenues provided through which to exert pressures.

In an attempt to gain a feeling for how receptive the
libraries were to programs which mandate citizen participation, [18] data were collected for each of the responding service areas on the availability of Model Cities and Office of
Economic Opportunity, Community Action Program funds. [19]
Ninety-nine of the service areas received either Model
Cities or Community Action Program funds, and 27 of the 99
received funds from both programs; however, only 18 libraries reported Model Cities and Community Action programs as possible avenues for citizen participation in library

affairs, and only two reported both programs.

e.   Branch Library Advisory Groups

Libraries with at least one branch, 118 in this study,[20] were asked to indicate whether any of its branches had a specially formed branch library advisory group or board. Fifteen of the libraries (17 percent) reported that at least one of their branches had such a group or board. All of these libraries had at least three branches but only four of the libraries reported that more than one branch had such a group or board. Of these four libraries, all had at least nine branches.

One library reported having substantially more advisory groups than any of the other reporting libraries. Although it reported no branch library advisory groups, it indicated that it had 30 storefront libraries, each of which was advised by a community group.

f.   Decision Arenas in Which Citizens Participate

In Figure IA the degree to which citizens participate in the various decision-making arenas is included in the "other" category. Table 18 below, gives this information, as well as the information included in Figures IB and II, in a more precise form.

Obviously, citizens are not actively involved in many of the decisions which libraries must make. They are most actively involved in the planning of library programs, but it is impossible to determine from this data how citizen input effects the planning process and final program design. (Again, whether or not citizens should be involved in any of these or any other decision-making arenas is not in question

TABLE 18:   EXTENT TO WHICH CITIZENS
PARTICIPATE IN DECISION ARENAS

Decision Arena	Frequency	Percent
Personnel:		
Selecting head librarian	1	. 8%
Selecting professionals	1	. 8
Selecting non-professionals	1	. 8
Determining salaries	1	. 8
Determining promotions	1	. 8
Budget Preparation	2	1. 5
Materials Selection	10	7. 5
Program Planning	38	28. 2
Facilities:		
Building Design	9	6. 8
Site Selection	12	9. 1
Across all decision arenas: (% average)		5. 7%

at this point.   Citizen participation objectives are discussed
in the Preface and Chapter I, and a discussion of citizen
participation objectives in libraries follows in Chapter 4 of
this study.)

g.   Attitudes of Reporting Librarians Toward
Citizen Participation

A summated rating scale was constructed for the
questionnaire responses in order to assess librarians' attitudes toward involving citizens in the decision-making process.   The original scale contained eight items; an analysis
of variability in the responses to the scale showed three
items to lack discriminatory power; e. g., to the statement:
"Citizen participation must be sought for ALL library decisions, without restriction" the responses were as follows:
Agree strongly, 2; Agree, 3; No opinion, 4; Disagree, 81;
and Disagree strongly, 42.   Because so little variability in
response was shown, these results were removed from the

attitude analysis, as were the responses to the statements:
"Library effectiveness could be improved through greater
communication with those its service is intended to benefit"
(115 respondents replied on the agree end of the continuum),
and "A significant number of citizens are motivated to participate in library policy making" (109 respondents replied
on the disagree end of the continuum).

Five statements remained in the attitude toward citizen participation scale. These statements were:

(1) People have a clear idea of the types of services
the public library offers.

(2) Increased citizen participation in library policy
making causes more problems than its worth.

(3) Citizen participation must NEVER enter into the
area of administration.

(4) Special boards (or other mechanisms) should be
provided through which citizens may express
their opinions regarding public services.

(5) Library effectiveness could be improved through
more active participation of citizens in library
policy making.

The response values were first summed and then divided by the appropriate number of responses for each case.
Cases in which fewer than three statements were responded
to with an opinion were eliminated from the analysis. Last-
ly, the responses were categorized into a trichotomy of receptive, hesitant and resistant.

The results of a simple frequency/percentage analysis of the responses are given below in Table 19. Based
upon the results of the author's scale only, over 50 percent
of the responding librarians have a rather strong negative
attitude toward citizen participation and slightly over 70 percent have less than a positive attitude toward citizen partici-

TABLE 19: CITIZEN PARTICIPATION ATTITUDE SCALE

Attitude Category	Frequency	Percent
Receptive	35	29. 3%
Hesitant	22	18. 4
Resistant	62	52. 3
	119	100. 0%

pation.

Survey participants were asked to respond to these
statements from their personal point of view and since all
of the respondents were either library directors or members
of the key administrative staff, e. g., deputy or assistant directors, the scale taps the attitudes of high-level administrators only, and not library staffs or professional librarians
in general. (One library indicated that the library's professional staff had been polled to arrive at responses; this case
was eliminated from the analysis.) However, leaders often
set the style or tone for acceptable employee attitudes within an organization and, as has been demonstrated by the
findings in the policy making style section of this survey,
libraries exhibit a tendency to be hierarchical in nature.

One dimension of an institution's opportunity/con-
straint environment (i. e., those factors which come to bear
upon what an institution is or is not able to effect in terms
of its resources, objectives, etc.) is the attitude of its top
level administration toward ... (whatever may be the concern at hand). The attitude dimension becomes increasingly
important as that concern enters more closely into the
operational domain of top-level administration itself. For
example, a head librarian's general attitude toward automa-
tion plays a part in a library's decision to consider auto-
mating the activities of the library's acquisitions department;

however, his attitude toward an activity such as forms of
citizen participation which will directly effect the style of
management of the library will play a more central role in
the decision outcome.   Because the attitude toward citizen
participation expressed by top-level administrators plays an
important role in the capacity of public libraries to experiment with (or even consider) non-traditional forms of citizen
participation in the policy making process, the attitude scale
was used as a base from which to examine a number of the
other factors for which data was obtained in the survey. [21]

One factor which seems of interest is the number of
branch libraries which a library maintains.   Table 20 sum-
marizes the relationship between citizen participation attitude
and number of branch libraries.   As an institution's physical facilities increase in number, it seems reasonable that
administrators will seek management devices to aid in administrative tasks.   While this table demonstrates that as number of branch libraries increases so does the percent of administrators who express receptive attitudes toward citizen
participation, still, less than half of the administrators of
the largest public libraries express a receptive attitude
toward citizen participation.   Apparently, citizen participation is not notably considered to be a helpful management
tool in libraries, regardless of the degree to which the institution is physically decentralized.

In looking at factors which obtain directly to citizen
participation, it is reasonable to expect that libraries whose
administrators profess a more enthusiastic attitude toward
citizen participation would also be those which provide the
most opportunities for citizen participation.   Tables 21
through 23 outline the results of examining citizen participation attitude with three opportunity factors.

TABLE 20: CITIZEN PARTICIPATION ATTITUDE BY
NUMBER OF BRANCH LIBRARIES STRATA

| Branch Strata Cases | Citizen Participation Attitude | | | Total |
	Receptive	Hesitant	Resistant	
(27) No branches	18. 5%	29. 6%	51. 9%	100. 0%
(23) 1-2	17. 4	17. 4	65. 2	100. 0
(32) 3-8	37. 5	9. 4	53. 1	100. 0
(28) 9-24	35. 7	17. 9	46. 4	100. 0
(9) 25- +	44. 4	22. 2	33. 3	100. 0
Total	29. 4%	18. 5%	52. 1%	100. 0%
Cases	(35)	(22)	(62)	(119)

TABLE 21: CITIZEN PARTICIPATION ATTITUDE BY
REPORTED AVAILABILITY OF CITIZEN PARTICIPATION
OPPORTUNITIES

| Citizen Participation Opportunities Cases | Citizen Participation Attitude | | | Total |
	Receptive	Hesitant	Resistant	
(33) Available	52. 9%	18. 2%	18. 6%	28. 7%
(82) Unavailable	47. 1	81. 8	81. 4	71. 3
Total	100. 0%	100. 0%	100. 0%	100. 0%
Cases	(34)	(22)	(59)	(115)

TABLE 22: CITIZEN PARTICIPATION ATTITUDE BY
EXISTENCE OF BRANCH LIBRARY ADVISORY GROUPS

| Branch Library Advisory Groups Cases | Citizen Participation Attitude | | | Total |
	Receptive	Hesitant	Resistant	
(37) Have Groups	46. 9%	43. 7%	30. 6%	38. 1%
(60) No Groups	53. 1	56. 3	69. 4	61. 9
Total	100. 0%	100. 0%	100. 0%	100. 0%
Cases	(32)	(16)	(49)	(97)

Table 21 shows the expected relationship, i.e., a receptive attitude towards citizen participation accompanies opportunities created for it more often than not; however, the
difference in percentages (53 available, 47 unavailable) is
certainly not striking. Those librarians which professed

TABLE 23: CITIZEN PARTICIPATION ATTITUDE BY
NUMBER OF DECISION ARENAS IN WHICH CITIZEN GROUPS
ARE MENTIONED AS ACTIVE

Number of Decision Arenas	Citizen Participation Attitude			
	Receptive	Hesitant	Resistant	Total
Cases				
(37) At least one	42.9%	27.3%	25.8%	31.1%
(82) None	57.1	72.7	74.2	68.9
Total	100.0%	100.0%	100.0%	100.0%
Cases	(35)	(22)	(62)	(119)

either hesitant or resistant attitudes were more clearly able
to work in an opportunity environment which reflects their
attitudes toward citizen participation.

In Tables 22 and 23 a professed receptive attitude
does not translate into specific instances of citizen participation in terms of having branch library advisory groups or
involving citizen groups in areas of library policy decision-
making. In fact, as respondents were asked to cite increasingly more specific incidents of citizen participation, those
administrators who claimed to favor citizen participation
were less able to translate their preference into reality.

Although the results of all three tables show the receptive group as indeed being somewhat more inclined to
provide opportunities for citizen participation, it appears
that regardless of the attitude expressed by the top level administrators, at least in terms of the scale devised to
measure their attitude, citizen participation is a factor of
little importance in public library policy making.

Table 24, which follows, shows that the administrators' expressed attitudes toward citizen participation and
their responses to the diagrams which illustrate types of internal decision-making flow are complementary; i.e., when
library administrators have a receptive attitude toward par-

ticipation of citizen groups in library policy making, participative internal decision-making processes are more often
likely to be employed. Still, evidence from the relationship
shown gives only little support to the contention that a library's participative internal decision-making structure provides a receptive environment for citizen participation. In
light of what has been identified in library literature22 as
professional self-consciousness due to the profession's relative youth--i.e., that it is still trying to carve out for itself
its precise occupational territory--it is perhaps understandable that only those persons who are credentialed and experienced, or those who bring to the environment other well-
defined occupational expertise, e.g., lawyers, are those
from whom decision-making input is sought.

TABLE 24: POLICY MAKING STYLE BY CITIZEN PARTICIPATION ATTITUDE

Citizen Participation Attitude Cases	Policy Making Style				
	Author-itative	Cooper-ative	Integra-tive	Partici-pative	Total
(34) Receptive	5. 9%	50. 0%	. 0%	44. 1%	100. 0%
(22) Hesitant	18. 2	50. 0	4. 5	27. 3	100. 0
(55) Resistant	34. 5	36. 4	5. 5	23. 6	100. 0
Total	22. 5%	43. 3%	3. 6%	30. 6%	100. 0%

Tables 25 and 26 examine two questions relating to
the libraries' service policies in conjunction with citizen participation attitude. It is perhaps reasonable to expect that
libraries which wish to include, or are at least receptive to
the idea of including, citizens as participants in the policy
making process may also be more actively concerned with
the informational needs of citizens. Although the question
on library goals demonstrated problems of reliability and

validity, when examined in relationship to citizen participation attitude the expected relationship is evident. (See the
following section of this chapter for explanatory material relating to the service policy orientation categories.)

TABLE 25: CITIZEN PARTICIPATION ATTITUDE BY
ORIENTATION OF LIBRARY SERVICE POLICY

Service Policy Orientation	Citizen Participation Attitude			Total
	Receptive	Hesitant	Resistant	
Cases				
(32) Information	44. 1%	40. 0%	16. 1%	29. 1%
(78) Traditional	55. 9	60. 0	83. 9	70. 9
Total	100. 0%	100. 0%	100. 0%	100. 0%
Cases	(34)	(20)	(56)	(110)

When the respondents were asked a more specific question
relating to information services, i. e., whether or not the library maintained a community information file (See Table
26), the relationship between a receptive attitude and the
provision of an information file becomes more evident than
the similar relationship expressed in Table 25.

TABLE 26: CITIZEN PARTICIPATION ATTITUDE BY
EXISTENCE OF A COMMUNITY INFORMATION FILE

Community Information File	Citizen Participation Attitude			Total
	Receptive	Hesitant	Resistant	
Cases				
(30) No	8. 6%	40. 9%	29. 5%	25. 4%
(88) Yes	91. 4	59. 1	70. 5	74. 6
Total	100. 0%	100. 0%	100. 0%	100. 0%
Cases	(35)	(22)	(61)	(118)

h. Summary

Based upon the findings of the citizen participation
portion of this survey it appears that citizen participation in

public library policy making is quite minimal, with the exception of the role of the library board. Even with reference to one of the library's traditional forms of citizen participation, the Friends of the Library, only slightly over 32 percent of the libraries involved citizens outside of the library board in their policy making process. Restricting the analysis to non-traditional forms, 17 percent of the libraries had at least one branch library advisory group and 28 percent stated that there was some form of program available through which citizens could participate in the library's policy making.

Service Policy Orientation

A number of questions were asked in order to determine the general orientation of the service policy of the libraries. The intent was to try to determine whether a library thought of its goals in terms of information services or materials (i.e., traditional) services; however, the discriminatory capacity of the measures used to make this categorization are rather insensitive, due to the nature of the questions asked. In four of the five questions included in this portion of the questionnaire, my judgment of what is fundamentally an information service and what is in essence a materials service was the sole criterion for placing a specific library in one category or the other. For example, in response to the question, "Does the library as a whole or any of its branches in particular have specific library services or programs which you consider innovative?" if the respondent answered yes, and then described a "book delivery service to shut-ins," this service was not considered information-oriented; if, on the other hand, the service or pro-

gram described was "providing drug information pamphlets
in drug clinics" or "consultant and referral services on tax,
legal, medical and social welfare problems, " the service
was considered to be information-oriented. In arriving at
the proper classification for each library, I took considerable care to give an information classification to any service
which could even remotely be classified as such, while at
the same time guarding to see that not every library program became information-oriented.

Admittedly, the results of this portion of the survey
should be accepted only with reservations, for in addition to
the four questions with open-ended answers which I classified, it should be remembered that the question on the ranking of the library's service goal priorities showed itself to
produce the least reliable and valid responses. Nonetheless,
it is felt that at least a general picture of the service orientation of these libraries can be achieved through the measures
used in this analysis. In no case should the analysis be
construed to imply that a library is definitely information-
oriented in all of its services or definitely materials-oriented,
but rather that a library appears to tend toward either information or materials-oriented services (i. e., traditional library services).

a.   Ranking of Service Goal Priorities

One hundred twenty-one libraries responded to the
question on service goal priorities. Of these, 35 (29 percent)
were classified as information-oriented. A library was considered to have information-oriented goal priorities if it
ranked three of the following five goals among its first five
ranks:

(1) to enhance individual opportunities for self-devel-
     opment
(2) to assist people in their daily occupations
(3) to provide information about community activities
(4) to aid and supplement formal educational programs
(5) to provide the opportunity for the direct commu-
     nication of ideas on important problems.

In addition, a small number of libraries included in the open-
ended category for this question indicated that their only goal
was to provide information to their service area residents;
these libraries also were classified as information-oriented.

   b.   Innovative Information Programs

     Over half of the responding libraries, 55 percent (i. e.,
69 of 125), considered that they had "innovative" library programs.   Twenty-eight of these libraries described at least
one program with what appeared to be an information-orientation.   The most often mentioned programs were:

TABLE 27:   INNOVATIVE INFORMATION PROGRAMS

Program	Frequency
Outreach	10
Drug Information	7
Information and Referral	7
Special Interest Programs:	
e. g., cooking, auto repair	5
Language classes (staff and user)	2
Community profiles	2

     Of course, it may be that many information-oriented
libraries do not consider their library programs to be innovative.   As one respondent put it, "I've been in this biz 21
years; there isn't much that I consider innovative, though
it's polite to pretend. "   (It is interesting to note that this

library was one of those classified as information-oriented
on the ranking of goal priorities.) Also, it is difficult to
determine from the word "outreach" just how information-
oriented a program might be; however, it was felt that it
would be best to assume that the programs were more than
simply providing additional access points to books and magazines.

The results on this question, 22 percent information-
oriented, correspond well with the results on the goal orientation question in which 29 percent were classified as information-oriented.   A sub-analysis of these two questions
showed that 24 of the 35 libraries classified as information-
oriented on the goal priority question were also classified
as information-oriented on the innovative programs question.

c.   Community Information File

Three-quarters of the libraries reported that they
maintained community information files; 99 of 131 libraries,
or 76 percent.   In describing the purpose and use of these
files, 51 (39 percent) clearly indicated that the file was
created for use by both library users and library staff.   A
small number of respondents (10) described local history
collections as their community information files; these libraries were not classified as having the type of community
information file which is intended to provide current and accurate information to library users.

d.   Types of Service the Library Should Offer

In an attempt to gain a clearer picture of what services the respondents thought the library should offer, they
were asked to describe what kinds of services had been re-

quested during the last year which the library should NOT
offer. (For a list of the types of services requested, see
Table 16, in which responses to this question are presented
in another context.) The purpose of this question was to
gain a different perspective on library service by seeing
whether citizen groups request information-type services,
e.g., referral, discussion groups, or local information files,
but are denied them on the grounds that it is inappropriate
for the library to offer such service; however, only 32 libraries (25 percent of the respondents to the question) indicated that citizen groups had requested inappropriate services, and only four of these stated that either discussion
groups or referral services were not appropriate. The
dearth of citizen groups requests, coupled with the large
variety of inappropriate services reported by the respondents,
make it difficult to analyze the question from the point of
view of its original intent.

To gain a further perspective on what services the
library should offer, respondents were asked to identify services which other community agencies were offering and that
they thought the library should be offering. Twenty of the
127 libraries which responded to this question indicated that
there were such services. Sixteen libraries mentioned information and referral services; the four others cited such
reading related services as training adult illiterates.

e. Summary

Although the results of this portion of the survey are
hardly conclusive, it seems reasonable to say that these libraries tend to be rather firmly set in their orientation
toward traditional library service. A small number of

these libraries are concerned with providing community information files and feel that information and referral services are within the purview of the public library; in general,
however, they are a small number of the total respondents
and barely constitute what could be called a visible shift or
extension of library service goals.

Descriptive Analyses Summary

The descriptive analyses of this survey data show libraries as tending to be:

(1) Centralized in decision-making style;
(2) Inactive in citizen participation matters; and,
(3) Oriented toward traditional library service goals.

These are certainly not unexpected findings, [23] although the
number of libraries which tended toward these characteristics
is rather larger than I expected. Based upon this survey's
findings, the American public library appears to be quite a
stable insitution in this time of increased tolerance for experimentation and change in decision-making styles and institutional programming. While other public service agencies,
notably public school systems, police departments, public
welfare agencies and even city halls themselves, have been
experimenting both with forms of decentralized management
and with forms of citizen participation, ranging from simple
program planning communication and advice to and from citizens through full community control, it appears that the public library has been less sensitive and/or imaginative in its
approach to these areas. [24] In terms of the responsibility
or accountability of public service professionals to their
clientele, it seems essential that at least the leaders of the
profession must keep abreast of experimental and innovative

forms of management. While the data at hand do not allow
a categorical statement that the library profession's leaders
are less cognizant of management innovation than leaders of
other public service professions, it appears reasonable to
say that they are certainly not members of the cutting edge.

Investigation of the Principal Questions

One of the major purposes of the survey analysis was
to investigate whether a decentralized policy making style
tends to be found in association with an active citizen participation pattern; and further, to see if libraries that tend to
have an active citizen participation pattern view their service
goal priorities differently (e.g., as tending toward an information-orientation) from libraries that tend to have an inactive citizen participation pattern. It is to that purpose that
this study now turns.

Scales on each of the three variables were constructed
so that the associations of concern could more readily be investigated. The relationships between the two sets of variables were investigated by means of the rank order statistic,
Kendall's Tau b, computed from a categorization of the variables into six-part classifications. (This division of scores
is skewed slightly in favor of decentralization, active citizen
participation and information-oriented service priorities, and
is thus a conservative influence on the suggested direction
of the outcome.) These six-part classifications are given
below in Table 28.

TABLE 28:   POLICY STYLE, CITIZEN PARTICIPATION
AND SERVICE ORIENTATION SCORES:
SIX-PART CATEGORIZATION

Variable	Category	Scores	Frequency
Policy Style	Highly Decentralized	1.00-1.19	1
	Decentralized	1.20-1.39	4
	Moderately Decentralized	1.40-1.59	41
	Moderately Centralized	1.60-1.79	35
	Centralized	1.80-1.99	46
	Highly Centralized	2.00	5
Citizen	Highly Active	1.00-1.19	9
Participation	Active	1.20-1.39	27
	Moderately Active	1.40-1.59	22
	Moderately Inactive	1.60-1.79	38
	Inactive	1.80-1.99	27
	Highly Inactive	2.00	9
Service	High Information Orien-		
Orientation	tation	1.00-1.19	2
	Information Orientation	1.20-1.39	17
	Moderate Information		
	Orientation	1.40-1.59	30
	Moderate Traditional		
	Orientation	1.60-1.79	55
	Traditional Orientation	1.80-1.99	21
	High Traditional Orien-		
	tation	2.00	7

Decentralized Policy-Making and Citizen Participation

When the scores on the two variables are divided into a six-part categorization, Table 29 shows the results.

Based upon the descriptive analyses and this statistical measure, it is apparent that libraries which tend to a
decentralized policy making style do not, to a significant degree, also tend to have active citizen participation patterns.
In only one case was a library reported to be both highly
decentralized in its policy making style and highly active in

TABLE 29:   POLICY MAKING STYLE/CITIZEN
PARTICIPATION PATTERN: SIX-PART CATEGORIZATION

| Policy Making Style | Citizen Participation Pattern | | | | | | |
	Highly Active	Active	Moderately Active	Moderately Inactive	Inactive	Highly Inactive	
Centralized	1	0	0	3	0	1	5
Highly-Centralized	5	7	11	14	9	0	46
Moderately-Centralized	1	12	4	14	3	1	35
Moderately-Decentralized	0	8	7	7	13	6	41
Decentralized	1	0	0	0	2	1	4
Highly-Decentralized	1	0	0	0	0	0	1
	9	27	22	38	27	9	132

Kendall's Tau b for this table is .127; not a significant relationship.

its citizen participation pattern.

Citizen Participation and Service Policy Orientation

When the scores on the variables citizen participation pattern and service policy orientation are divided into the six-part categorization, the results are shown in Table 30.

Based upon the descriptive analyses and the statistical measure, it is apparent that libraries which tend to have an active citizen participation do not, to a significant degree, also tend to have information-oriented service policies.   In only two cases were libraries reported to be both highly active in their citizen participation pattern and highly oriented towards information services.

TABLE 30:   CITIZEN PARTICIPATION PATTERN/SERVICE
ORIENTATION: SIX-PART CATEGORIZATION

Citizen Partici- pation Pattern	Service Policy Orientation						
	High Infor- mation	Infor- mation	Low Infor- mation	Low Tradi- tion	Tradi- tion	High Tradi- tion	
Highly Inactive	0	1	1	4	2	1	9
Inactive	0	3	7	14	3	0	27
Moderately Inactive	0	6	9	15	5	3	38
Moderately Active	0	2	6	6	6	2	22
Active	0	3	5	14	4	1	27
Highly Active	2	2	2	2	1	0	9
	2	17	30	55	21	7	132

Kendall's Tau b for this table is -.042; not a significant relationship.

Summary

The questions which prompted and served to focus
this investigation--1) do public libraries characterized by
decentralized decision-making in their internal organizational
structure tend to have a higher degree of citizen participation in the determination of library policies than libraries
characterized by centralized decision-making? and 2) do public libraries characterized by an active citizen participation
pattern in the determination of library policies tend to view
their service goal priorities differently from libraries characterized by an inactive citizen participation pattern?--have
been investigated.   Due to the elusiveness of the factors
being studied, the somewhat imprecise data that was collected by means of the survey questionnaire, and the apparently rare incidences in the public library environment

of the factors being investigated, a _firm_ conclusion as to the
usefulness of these questions in helping to understand the
role of citizen participation in public libraries is difficult to
advance. (Recommendations for further research in the area
of citizen participation in the public library environment are
advanced in Chapter 5.) The major conclusion reached from
the survey data is simply that citizen participation in any
form other than the traditional library board is a phenomenon which has not impacted the public library to any significant degree. One could surmise from the survey findings
that librarians feel that library boards are the only necessary and proper avenue for citizen participation and that
they feel the traditional library board member is a credible
and sufficient representative of either their service area
constituency, or at least of their user group. Perhaps librarians feel complacent in this era of increased interest in
participatory management because they have traditionally had
citizen boards; but the data which has been collected does
not allow for any firm conclusions of an explanatory nature.

It is my opinion, corroborated with evidence gathered
by others cited in this study, notably Bundy and Wasserman
and Blasingame, that library leaders tend to be highly cautious in their administrative style. Professionalism, as I
understand it, demands critical--that is, evaluative--vision
from its leaders. Major public libraries might do well to
employ ombudsman-type partners in leadership, whose only
responsibility is to the people whom the library seeks to
serve, and whose only role is to pursue answers to questions such as: what are the things the library is trying to
do; and, from the vantage point of the library's clientele,
can the library's leaders be trusted in terms of values,
competence and spirit?

A major purpose in undertaking the survey reported
in this chapter was to identify libraries in which citizen
participation was being employed so that case study sites
could be chosen which would in fact yield the data of interest.   The case study method is considered to be the best
suited method to explore the complex of factors which may
bear upon the utilization of citizen participation in public libraries because it allows for in-depth scrutiny of elusive
and sensitive factors as obtained in citizen participation environments.   Although the survey identified only nine libraries with highly active citizen participation patterns, it
was felt that case studies would prove to be a worthwhile
complement to the survey and, further, would reveal factors
that could be investigated in a future, less exploratory,
study.

Choice of the Case Study Site(s)

The original design for this research called for a
small number of case studies (4 to 12).   It was expected
that the survey data analyses would demonstrate that a
limited though sufficient number of libraries (10-15) would
exhibit a high degree of participatory management coupled
with both an active citizen participation pattern and an information-oriented service policy.   In fact, only two libraries did.   (The distribution of case frequencies by high
and low categories on the three principal variables is given
below in Table 31.)   Further, as the table demonstrates,
82 cases were categorized as low on all three variables,
while 48 cases showed combinations of high and low categorizations on the variables.   As opposed to studying one case
from each of the variable combinations, it appeared advis-

able to look more closely at the exceptional or deviant cases, i.e., those cases categorized as high on the three principal variables.

TABLE 31:   CASE FREQUENCY DISTRIBUTION
ON THE THREE PRINCIPAL VARIABLES

	Variables		
Policy Style	Citizen Participation Pattern	Service Orientation	
High	High	High	2
High	High	Low	0
High	Low	High	1
High	Low	Low	2
Low	High	High	5
Low	High	Low	29
Low	Low	High	11
Low	Low	Low	82
			132

In an item-by-item comparison of the questionnaires of the two cases, one of the libraries consistently appeared to be the more exceptional case.   For example, it reported having substantially more branch library advisory groups; on the decision-making matrix it reported by far the most decision arenas having active citizen group involvement, and its library board was the most highly representative of its service area constituency in terms of the socially descriptive criteria investigated.   On the basis of the comparison analysis, it was decided to confine the case study phase of the research to this one library.

The case study is based primarily on interviews conducted at the site.   The interviews were unstructured in order to encourage free discussion, but were focused upon the following areas of concern:

(1) description in terms of formal and social representation of the citizen groups;

(2) extent of influence and power of citizen groups in the policy making process;

(3) degree to which the interviewees are able to verbalize an understanding of citizen participation objectives in the abstract;

(4) whether interviewees are able to detail objectives for citizen participation in the library's environment;

(5) expression of a general attitude toward citizen participation as an input into the policy making process; and

(6) evidence forwarded or perceptions expressed of the effects of citizen participation on the library's policy making process and/or service goals.

The intent of the case study was to discover what appear to be major factors in this particular library environment which promote either actual incidences of citizen participation, and/ or a philosophy of receptivity toward citizen participation in the policy making process. It is assumed that by bringing to light such factors in one library environment, extrapolations to other library environments may be made so that intelligence bearing upon the use of citizen participation inputs in the policy making process of public libraries may be increased.

Notes

1. Although studies such as Edwin E. Olson's Survey of the User Service Policies in Indiana Libraries and Information Centers (Indiana Library Studies, Report 10, 1970), Eric ED044139, investigate library policies, they do not focus upon the process involved in reaching policy decisions.

2. The literature bearing upon this assumption is volumi-
    nous. The following are those drawn upon most
    heavily by this author: C. J. Lammers, "Power and
    Participation in Decision-making in Formal Organiza-
    tions, " American Journal of Sociology, LXXIII (Sep-
    tember, 1967), pp. 201-216; Rensis Likert, The Hu-
    man Organization: Its Management and Value (New
    York: McGraw-Hill, 1967); Aaron Lowin, "Partici-
    pative Decision Making: A Model, Literature Critique
    and Prescriptions for Research, " Organizational Be-
    havior and Human Performance, III (1968), pp. 68-
    106; and, Nicos P. Mouzelis, Organization and Bu-
    reaucracy (Chicago: Aldine, 1960).

3. For example, see Henry J. Schmandt, Decentralization:
    A Structural Imperative (Washington, D.C.: Center
    for Governmental Studies, 1970).

4. Likert, op. cit. , p. 14.

5. Mildred L. Batchelder, Public Library Trustees in the
    Nineteen-Sixties (Chicago: American Library Asso-
    ciation, 1969), p. 51.

6. The most notable of the studies are: Batchelder, op.
    cit.; Oliver Garceau, The Public Library in the Po-
    litical Process (New York: Columbia University Press,
    1949); Carleton B. Joeckel, The Government of the
    American Public Library (Chicago: University of Chi-
    cago Press, 1935); Donald W. Koepp, Decision Mak-
    ing for the Public Library Function of Municipal Gov-
    ernment (Berkeley: University of California, 1966:
    Ph.D. Dissertation); Morton Kroll, Public Libraries
    of the Pacific Northwest (Seattle: University of Wash-
    ington Press, 1960); and Virginia G. Young, The Li-
    brary Trustee (New York: Bowker, 1969).

7. Batchelder, op. cit. , p. 5.

8. Paul E. Peterson, "Forms of Representation: Partici-
    pation of the Poor in the Community Action Program, "
    American Political Science Review, LXIV (June 1970),
    pp. 491-92.

9. Ibid. , p. 492.

10. U. S. Bureau of the Census, County and City Data

Book, 1967. (Washington, D.C.: Government Printing Office, 1968), Table 2, column 25 and Table 4,
column 228.

11. Ibid., Table 2, column 10, and Table 4, column 208.

12. Ibid., Table 2, column 15, and Table 4, column 212.

13. Of course, it is difficult to determine whether any spe-
     cific housewife is more appropriately classified as
     traditional or non-traditional; however, since they
     have historically served on library boards, the tradi-
     tional classification seems the most appropriate for
     those persons designated as housewife. Further, had
     the person had a job other than housewife, it is prob-
     ably safe to assume that her occupation would have
     been given on the questionnaire.

14. One of the 111 libraries which provided information on
     the racial composition of their library boards (not in-
     cluded in the above analysis) reported one board mem-
     ber as of Mexican-American heritage. No libraries
     reported Oriental board members.

15. The boards ranged in size from four (4) to 27 members
     with the median board size as seven (7).

16. See Joeckel, op. cit.

17. Mary Lee Bundy and Paul Wasserman, The Public Li-
     brary Administrator and His Situation; one part of the
     Executive Study Portion of a Program of Research in-
     to the Identification of Manpower Requirements, the
     Educational Preparation and the Utilization of Man-
     power in the Library and Information Profession.
     (College Park: University of Maryland, School of Li-
     brary and Information Services, June 1970), p. 68.

18. This is, of course, a very crude and non-discriminat-
     ing measure. Any number of factors other than non-
     receptivity to citizen participation might account for
     why a library did not indicate that the programs were
     available channels for citizen participation in their
     service areas. The details are provided only to indi-
     cate that the programs are indeed available, but were
     not perceived to be avenues for citizen participation
     in library affairs by the respondents to this survey.

19. Sources for this data were: for Model Cities, <u>HUD News</u>, March 26, 1970; for Community Action Programs, U.S. Office of Economic Opportunity, <u>Community Action Agency Atlas</u>, 3rd ed. (Washington, D.C.: May 1971). Further, a U.S. Department of Housing and Urban Development Internal memo on library programs in Model Cities (Washington, D.C.: October 1970) lists 16 of the 150 Model Cities as receiving funds for library related programs. Four of these cities were included in the sample for this study, of which two responded.

20. As was mentioned earlier, 14 of the libraries in this study are headquarters libraries for library systems. Because the relationship between a system headquarters library and its members appears to be significantly different from the relationship between a central library and its branches in terms of autonomy in decision-making, these 14 libraries are not included in this analysis of branch library advisory groups. Therefore, the base for the branch library advisory group analysis is 90 libraries.

21. Three rank order statistical measures, Gamma, Tau-C, and Somers D were obtained from the computer program used for the data analyses; i.e., the Northwestern University Cross Variable Analysis Program, NUCROS. The statistical results showed only limited relationships between the factors.

22. Documentation supporting this statement is given in Chapter 4 in which professionalism is further discussed.

23. Bundy and Wasserman, <u>op. cit.</u>, pp. 68-71, reach the same conclusions based upon their data.

24. For example, an analysis of bibliographies relevant to citizen participation and decentralized decision-making such as: U.S. Department of Housing and Urban Development, <u>Citizen and Business Participation in Urban Affairs; a Bibliography</u> (Washington, D.C.: Government Printing Office, 1970); and Walter E. Clark, <u>Community Power and Decision-making: A Selective Bibliography</u> (Monticello, Ill.: Council of Planning Librarians, 1971), among a number of others, reveals less than a handful of entries which even discuss

the public library as a relevant institutional setting
for experimentation, to say nothing of entries devoted
to reports of actual occurrences of the phenomena of
interest.

Chapter 3

CITIZEN PARTICIPATION AT A LARGE URBAN LIBRARY

The Setting

C. P. City* sprawls out to meet the visitor like a
giant squid; it entangles and sucks the passerby into its core.
There, in the innards of the city's cultural center, the central library stands magnificently, a visual refutation of all
who would claim that it is a marginal institution. A trip
around the city adds credence to the stereotype of the present
urban environment: bad air, dirty streets, abandoned buildings juxtaposed to occasional gleaming steel tubes which
seem to feed on the rubble. The visible people of C. P.
City seem mostly old or young, ethnic or non-white; they
queue in front of the many public service outlets which dot
the city. Throughout the city, small branch libraries squat

---

*The case study site will not be identified for several
reasons, but principally because of the chief administrators'
desire (the author concurs) to allow the library "to be about
the library's business of serving the people." Some unique
and rather important characteristics (chiefly sociological) of
the library environment will not be discussed because it would
at once become obvious to those familiar with the urban library scene just which library was visited. The library is
somewhat of a cause célèbre in the field and although the
chief administrators and many of the professional staff expressed a belief in the importance of outside scrutiny to the
growth of the library, they prefer to be less of a fish bowl
than they are presently.

in parks or on once well-landscaped corner lots, and bookmobiles rumble through the city streets, signalling the live-
liest manifestation of the library in the city with the exception of the central library and its specialized clientele.

C. P. City has traditionally been characterized as a
city with a strong mayor-council form of government. Its
political history is one of immense tension, contained by non-
partisan politics and a tradition of not-too agressive reform.
There has been, for some time, a sufficient level of responsiveness by the city government to labor and minorities
that an excessive number of scandals, riots and other mani-
festations of urban malaise has been averted. The political
atmosphere of the city appears to contain a dogged will to
conquer the present economic and social decline of the city;
despite physical evidence to the contrary, the political forces
in C. P. City are determined to save the central city from
abandonment.

One of the chief means by which the city seeks its
maintenance is through programs involving well-publicized
doses of citizen participation by representatives of most of
the various factions in the city. Traditionally, small busi-
nessmen (the large corporations have avoided political involvement in the city, preferring roles in state and federal
politics) and special interest groups have played key roles in
city politics. Office of Economic Opportunity and Department
of Housing and Urban Development programs which mandate
citizen participation from grassroots groups are therefore
more readily accepted in C. P. City than in many other
places, because numerous concentrations of political power
have not and do not create a major source of threat within
the city's political environment. The city also has one of
the most receptive environments to decentralized officialdom;

i. e., little city halls and their mini-mayors have been instituted throughout the city.

The above factors in the city-wide political environment, i. e., receptivity to forms of decentralization and participatory management (including citizen participation), are
undoubtedly a major factor in the library's somewhat purpose-
ful drift toward these operational techniques. Equally important, however, are personnel changes in the library's top
administrative staff and library board membership in the
past several years.

The Actors

Although the mayor is the most powerful figure in the
city[1] and is <u>himself</u> not a friend of the library, [2] the top
level administration of the library has been able to maintain
the library's programs with only some curtailment in staff
and service. Presently and in the recent past, the city
council has counted among its members those who are either
themselves sympathetic to the library's continued existence[3]
or are responsive to the overtures of the Friends of the Library and especially to a citizens library lobby formed during a recent budget crisis. [4]

The top administrative level of the library (i. e., the
director, assistant director and library board) express, with
varying degrees of conviction, an ambiguous attitude towards
the continuing financial crisis of the library. While cutting
the budget is to a minor extent taken as a denial of their
personal capabilities and an assault on the appropriateness
of their sense of what is truly essential for the city's continued survival, they believe it has allowed the library to
take some necessary first steps toward the restructuring of

its staff and programs. The threat of additional library budget curtailment, while in no way warmly embraced, is certainly not about to panic them.

Library Board

The library board members are influential representatives of the major forces within the city's political environment: labor, women, and ethnic and racial groups as well
as the concerned white, upper socio-economic class.   The
members are blatantly middle-class professionals and have
progressed far beyond being apologetic for their condition.
While some of the board members are undoubtedly serving
for almost exclusively personal political advantage, for the
most part the board appears to believe deeply that the public library has an important role to play in the life of the
contemporary urban dweller.   The board is highly aware
that the C. P. City library is in the throes of attempting to
initiate profound changes; in fact, they feel that they have in
large part served as the impetus to change.   Especially
within the past three years, the board has been instrumental
in initiating change and some of its past and the majority
of its present members are the architects of the proposed
future of the library.   The library board has: 1) drawn to
the library top-level administrators whose vision of the library's role in the city is neither myopic nor rigid; 2) in-
sisted upon guarantees of fair employment practices by all
of the library's suppliers; 3) opened library board meetings
to all staff members and citizens and encouraged attendance;
4) occasionally sent open letters to all staff members ex-
plaining both mayor/city council actions and library board
activities;[5] and 5) was instrumental in the recent formation
of the Urban Library Trustees Council.

The library board is undoubtedly the group associated with the library which is most receptive to citizen participation. Each of the five members interviewed (the board consists of six members) expressed total receptivity to the idea of branch library advisory boards with powerful, though not necessarily veto, roles in the decision-making process for the branches. Further, the board members do not see the citizen participation approach to library management in a simplistic manner; because of their direct experiences with citizen participation in activities outside of their role as library board members, e.g., Model Cities and nation-wide religious, racial and labor organizations, they consider citizen participation to be problematic and largely inefficient, but nonetheless essential. 6

A few quotes from the interviews will illustrate what the board members think about citizen participation in library policy making:

> I have been advocating branch library boards for many years. But, they must have a clear understanding that their role is more than simply advisory. The librarians must understand this too.

> We are not experienced; they are experienced. We must learn from their experience so that the library can serve them.

> Library services are not comparable to either roller rinks or garbage collection. Libraries can be the life line of the city, if citizens are involved in their development and direction.

> Their primary role of the library ought to be the provision of essential information services for the citizens. By that I mean consumer information, income tax service and the like. Forms of information are the prerogative of the library; information is the prerogative of the people. They must be involved in the development of these services.

The Director

At the first meeting, the library director seems almost unbelievable. Anyone familiar with the typical[7] large public library administrator would concur. In no way meaning to detract from his qualities, it must be said that he would not have the position if it were not for the firm resolve of the majority of the library's board as it was constituted at the time of his appointment. Although many of the staff and concerned library users (particularly the Friends of the Library) reacted quite coolly to the appointment of the director, it became clear during the case study that their reactions were based largely on socio-political factors (such as fears of the redirection of the library's programs and the redefinition of the library's clientele) and not upon such factors as "lack of administrative experience" which was one of the major reasons for disapproval cited at the time of his appointment, and again during interviews with some professional staff members at the time of this case study. Although, in part, their fears of "radicalism" are justified, ironically, the director appears to be almost traditional in his attitudes toward the major goals of the library; this seems especially true when his attitudes are contrasted to those of the assistant director and the majority of the library board members. In essence, he sees the role of the library as increasing each city resident's ability in and enjoyment of reading. The purpose of this role, however, is not one of recreation, but rather is to enhance individual (especially non-traditional library clientele) opportunities for self-development. This apparently traditional attitude grows out of his feeling that the library must lay some groundwork for

its future mission by making itself more visible and viable
in the life of the communities within the city. He feels this
is necessary because of the protracted time prior to his administration when the library was in a period of virtual program and service stasis. This perception of his role as
groundworks architect contributes to his apparent traditional-
ism, although it may be more accurate to say that he is
simply a patient man rather than a traditional one.

Yet, with regard to citizen participation, the director
was somewhat hesitant to state a firm opinion. The branch
for which he suggested that a branch library advisory group
might serve as a pilot is one of the more affluent and heavily used branches. When asked about the possibility of experimenting with autonomous branch library boards, he voiced
reservations centering around the possible illegality of such
an approach in C. P. City. (Two library board members
saw no legal problems in instituting advisory boards for
branch libraries.) It is probable that neither autonomous,
i.e., direct control by a board representing a constituency
of less than the entire city, nor semi-autonomous, i.e., a
board accountable to the director and library board of the
library as a whole, branch library boards had been previously considered seriously by the director as an approach to
providing either a different or a better configuration of branch
library services.

The director showed intense enthusiasm for, though
limited knowledge about, the advisory groups which were reported to have played a part in the development of the storefront libraries in the city. This lack of specific knowledge
of the groups is attributable to the director's perception of
his role, and his belief in the full delegation of responsibil-

ity and authority where appropriate. His perception of the
director's role is one of facilitator of policy rather than
maker of policy. He has limited active involvement in the
daily operations of the library, but rather concentrates on
representing the library and the interests of its users and
potential users throughout the city. As he so succinctly
states his present role: "The problem of just staying alive
is so great!" Not a small amount of resignation can be de-
tected in his voice as he makes this statement, for he states
a preference for participating in the design and implementation of library programs; still, the director appears to be a
cautious person in relation to changes in the fundamental mode
of management and service orientation for the library.   This
is a most understandable position in view of the rather short
time he has been the top-level administrator, and also in
light of the present economic position of the city and thus of
the library. But, again, contrary to the fears of his de-
tractors, the director, perhaps or undoubtedly astutely, has
promoted only minor (though potentially fundamental) changes
in the present form of administration and focus of library
service; he believes that changes such as more open communications with the staff and increased involvement with the
community can begin to meet the needs of library staff and
city residents.

        The director's sense of his most important accom-
plishments to date are: 1) keeping the library sufficiently
funded by the city; 2) developing an active public relations
program; 3) decentralizing the library's decision-making process; 4) facilitating use of the library by greatly simplifying
(virtually disbanding) registration procedures; and 5) instituting required proof of fair employment practices by all library suppliers.   The factors which he feels have been the

most important for the realization of these accomplishments are the support and ideas of the library board, the interest of citizen groups, and the abilities of the assistant director.

Assistant Director

While the director's main responsibility is that of assuring the library's continued existence by maintaining effective relationships with the political powers and present groups of influentials in the city, the assistant director's responsibilities focus more on the internal organization and programs of the library; this is not to say that the assistant director does not play a role in the political activities of the library, for he does, especially with relation to state government functions, but his central area of responsibility relates to the library's daily operations.

The assistant director's tenure with the library is quite short, but within that time he has had an observable impact on the library's operations and programs according to those interviewed. With encouragement from the library board and approval from the director, the assistant director has opened to all library employees a direct channel of communication to the highest level of administration, i. e., any employee can see him directly at any time about any library-related concern. [8]   In addition to this informal communication channel, either instituted or emphasized by the assistant director, he has organized formal monthly meetings with non-supervisory and non-professional staff. These meetings are opened to all library employees in these classes regardless of whether they work in the central library or in one of the auxiliary facilities. [9]

The assistant director's view of library service is

rather different from that of the director and of the majority
of other persons interviewed (with the exception of the library board members).   Since his arrival he has continually
pressed for the development of a more central role in the
library's program for effective community information service.   It is his belief that community information service
should be the overriding priority for the library.   To that
end he has seen to the employment of a full-time staff member, who has during the past year been creating an information file for the city.   Federal monies have been obtained
to make this service operational before the close of 1972.
(Details of this service will be discussed below in the section on Information-Oriented Services.)

The assistant director is convinced that active citizen
participation in the form of branch library boards should be
a major means by which the library can re-direct its priorities.   He favors direct community control of some branches
as an effective form of branch library management.   (The
assistant director's concept of citizen participation as a
management form is a great contrast to the director's concept of citizen participation as a public relations technique.
Although his views on citizen participation and his support
by a majority of the library board are known among other
top level staff, the responsibility for branch and auxiliary library activity does not reside in the position of assistant director.)

The assistant director is a person of cool rationality
and infinite patience.   Although the changes he has initiated
during his tenure (i. e., increased staff participation in decision-making and an atmosphere of increased administrative
level tolerance for experimentation in library service and
programs) are potentially of great significance, and the po-

sitions which he espouses signal profound change in library
management and service, the extent to which they are being
embraced by the staff may be sufficient to stifle them.   On
the other hand, except for a minority of staff members, his
positions have not met with outright disapproval, and his
sense of the capacity for rate of change at the library, which
is the reason for his great patience, may be accurate.

Other Top-Level Staff

The perception of the goals of the public library by
the rest of the top-level staff is quite different from that of
the library board and the assistant director; it is more akin
to what the director perceives, but is certainly less flexible
and less well-defined.   These staff members are proud of
the vast and totally impressive central research library and
of the library's past growth.   They are highly facility- and
materials-oriented and are also extremely pleasant people.
Citizen participation in or control of branch libraries in the
form of branch library boards is not seen as a radically new
phenomenon because they genuinely believe that citizens already participate in the decision-making processes for branch
libraries.   If they could allow themselves to comprehend the
various goals of citizen participation, suggestions for participation and/or control would shake them to their very core,
but they manage to come away from a discussion of citizen
participation appearing either as though they understand or
as though they may contemplate it further.   They are the
wise incrementalists, [10] apparently enthusiastic about little
and afraid of nothing.   They appear to be representative of
the majority of the professional staff and, in my opinion,
pose the greatest barrier to change and perhaps threaten the

very continuance of branch library service in C. P. City.

  In relation to the concerns of this study one of the
top-level staff members plays the most significant role; he
is the head of the office for extension services. He is responsible for all branch library, storefront library, bookmobile, deposit station and extension services of the library.
He appears to be rather complacent, and understandably so,
for if one compares the types of programs and services of
this library to those of many other libraries, their extent
and diversity are truly great. Almost every public library
service that has ever been suggested is in some way in evidence in C. P. City. One modern branch is so thoughtfully
designed for the physically handicapped that in certain parts
of the building not being handicapped is a handicap. There
is service to prisons, schools, Head Start Programs, Model
Cities Neighborhood centers, little city-halls, shut-ins, un-
wed mothers' homes, senior citizens hotels, drug clinics,
boys' clubs, housing commission outlets, free schools and
neighborhood organization headquarters. The library has
certainly reached out with its traditional services; that it has
been rebuked in many of its efforts does not seem to have
been taken seriously, if indeed it has even been noticed.
No attempt at program evaluation has been undertaken, largely because it takes such gargantuan effort and real skill
simply to keep all the present programs and services running; however, program evaluation could be undertaken if the
assistant director for extension services dared to do so. It
appears that the try-one-of-everything approach is too well-
entrenched in the division at this point in time to reorient
the approach by disbanding some services and concentrating
on the quality of fewer services. The sheer magnitude of
the services offered through the division has served as an

effective barrier to evaluation and as a defense against criticism.

The assistant director of extension services has had the most direct contact with citizen groups over the past several years.   He seems hesitant in trying to distinguish between levels of involvement by citizen groups; for example, in his perception the Friends of the Library and the Model Cities Citizen Library Committee are more the same than they are different.   He, like the majority of the other professional staff interviewed, is so imbued with a rather omnipotent view of the responsibility of a professional that citizen participation is, by definition, simply a means by which professionals can receive information from and, more significantly, can send information to community groups.   He believes that citizen participation is a slow process of encouraging increased involvement with the library and is principally manifested in increased library use.   When asked to cite specific examples of citizen participation in library activities, simple requests for services phoned into the office by citizen groups were mentioned as the number one form of citizen participation.   No examples of the library making overtures to specific citizen groups was mentioned. (It was mentioned that many librarians, "of course, belong to local citizen groups. ")   The extension services office does not encourage citizen participation, in even this limited sense; it really only fills reasonable requests to the limits of its financial capacities.   Citizen participation does not mean giving citizens a role in the decision-making process; it is rather one part traditional public relations and one part "giving 'em what they want!"   There was no indication that citizen groups could be a source of intelligence for devising policy or could provide the base for a different form of library management.

One of the other professionals in this office appears
to have views substantially different from the office's director.   While the office director does not talk in terms of priorities or directions for the programs of the library, this
staff member has clearly formed opinions on the library's
purposes.   He feels that community control of a number of
branch libraries in C. P. City is a necessary step which
ought to be taken in the immediate future, and that locally
focused information services should be the major service
offered by branch libraries.   He is convinced that citizen
participation in the libraries of C. P. City does not need to
be encouraged; he argues, rather, that it must no longer be
contained.   The articulation of this point of view within the
office is difficult to hear over the din created by the furious
and largely undirected activity within the office.   But even if
this disparate point of view were openly stated, I believe
that it would be misunderstood, because the tenor of the office is such that new ideas are recast into traditional molds.

Branch Librarians

Four branch librarians were interviewed, each for at
least an hour's duration.   It was quite clear that even though
only one would openly admit that branch service at his library was more of a losing than a winning game, they all
felt (and believed that the majority of their colleagues felt)
that present branch library service was largely ineffective,
even for the present library users.   They all cited some
mildly successful programs that were presently offered; these
were all for children.   They all expressed faith in their
staff members, but were less enthused about the facilities

and materials available. They spent a great deal of time
selecting books even though they admitted that book circulation was low at their branch. (One of the librarians interviewed gave the distinct impression that he felt that one day
soon he would choose the book which would act as the key-
stone to his collection, and then community support of the
branch would be overwhelming.) Only one of the librarians
could offer any suggestions for improving library service at
his branch.

During the interviews all of the branch librarians
cited at least one example of citizen involvement in the activities of their branch. For the most part these were activities of the past. For example, "the citizens who initiated that program left the community," or "the organization
which had been involved has disbanded," and "the new administrator of the group is not so interested in the service
which the library is offering his group." The consensus of
the interviewed branch librarians was that the majority of
branch librarians in C. P. City are at the least knowledgeable about the groups and activities of their constituencies,
and not a few of them belong to a large number of community groups. They encourage local groups to use branch facilities for their meetings and by so doing, encourage them
to use library materials. They were candid in admitting
that their success in involving the library in community activities was rather minimal. None of the librarians interviewed suggested that the library might serve as an arm for
gathering intelligence for local community group concerns
and projects. Branch library involvement with community
groups is limited to the provision of materials and facilities
and does not include the provision of specialized reference
services. The branch librarians expressed little--positive

or negative--interest in obtaining either support or intelligence for new branch library services by means of branch library boards. I received the distinct feeling that the majority of those interviewed had never considered instituting branch library boards or that the librarians felt that it would be impossible to gather together enough people who could or would sustain their interest in playing such a role for a significant amount of time.

Only one branch librarian openly stated that "a radical change needs to take place in the services of this branch in order to justify its continued existence in this community." He had made a rough calculation that the "cost of each service transaction at this branch is $50.00." He feels that the branch might be turned over to the community for use at its disposal, and that professional librarians might suggest that it be used as a community information center.

Summary

In the report of the recently conducted Proposed Public Library Goals--Feasibility Study, the problem which was cited as the third most critical was "staff--inflexibility--lack of service orientation."[11] At the C. P. City library this problem is, in my opinion, the most critical. In contrast to the complaints I have heard from many librarians, that the top level administrators of public libraries are inflexible and cannot see that library services must change, the vision from the majority of the top at the C. P. City library is clearly toward a profound reorganization in both the management style and service orientation of the library. A massive barrier to change at this library is found at the middle management level--department heads and branch li-

brarians and their chief assistants.   The staff situation at
the C. P. City library is analogous to the analysis of poverty
program management forwarded by Robert C. Wood, who was
Secretary of Housing and Urban Development under President
Johnson.   "The new spirit of policy activism combined with
the old tradition of occupational provincialism is a disaster
for effective government. "[12]   Wood felt then that policy decisions made in Washington were being reinterpreted by low
or middle level professional staff, and that as a result,
either unintended or no change was taking place.   At the C.
P. City library, although the top level administration has
provided some direction for policy change, the professional
vision is so guarded that perception has not even taken place.
(Perhaps it is unfortunate that this library espouses non-
authoritarian decision-making; yet, even if the administration
of the library were to mandate change, the barrier is probably, as the assistant director perceives, presently too great.
But, perhaps too, the message from the top-level administration has not been strongly enough stated.)

        The most critical aspect of the staff problem at the
middle management level may be the abject lack of both
knowledge and understanding of the changes which have taken
place within: 1) the C. P. City environment; 2) the library;
and 3) the field of public librarianship in general.   It was
reported in the interviews, by the middle managers themselves, that their majority senses no basic change in the
philosophy of the library board or of the top-level administrators from that of the two past administrations.   Although
these middle managers are aware that the majority of their
constituency has changed in important socio-economic characteristics, and that they are now serving only a minority
of citizens (many of whom are non-city, non-tax supporting

suburban residents), these facts have no significant impact
upon either their view of their proper role or of the need
for their present services throughout the city.   Further, they
are uninformed of the experiments and programs which exist
or have taken place in other libraries.   Even the most widely publicized library activities have been overlooked; this is
true even of those who are the library's reported activists
and of those whose area of responsibility in the library is
narrow and tightly defined.   Although the C. P. City library
maintains an extensive professional library and some of its
staff are active in a variety of American Library Association
activities, there is little knowledge of service and management experimentation.   Perhaps the admonition of library
school professors, that the popular journals only contain
"how I done it good at X library" articles, has been taken
too much to heart by the C. P. City library's professional
staff members. [13]   Although it is important to realize that
one of the major findings gleaned from several decades of
social, political and economic studies focusing on cities is
that all cities have important characteristics which make them
unique from one another, it is equally important to understand that uniqueness alone does not mean that a successful
program in one city may not also be successful in another.
The lack of knowledge of other public library programs and
services is an indictment of the professional calibre of the
staff of any major library.

      A major roadblock to the provision of effective li-
brary service in C. P. City in the clearly visible, but pre-
sumably[14] not discussed, division of opinion among members
of the top level administration as to the proper goal or goals
of public library service.   This lack of goal specification accounts in part for the lack of program evaluation at the li-

brary. (Evaluation is after all extremely difficult, to say
nothing of embarrassing, when it is not clear what a program
hopes to achieve.) It appears that the library ought to undertake an evaluation of its priorities such as was discussed by
Larry Earl Bone.[15] An airing of the profound differences
which exist might well signal the end of branch library service in the city, but it might also provide a definition of purpose which is so obviously missing in present branch library
services. This conflict ought to be brought out into the open
or it may suffocate the library from within, before the mayor
is able to stifle it from without.

Citizen Participation in the Library's Programs

C. P. City library reported active citizen participation in all but two of the ten decision-making areas provided
on the survey questionnaire. The only areas in which citizens were reported as not participating actively were: 1) selection of the head librarian; and 2) determination of facility
design. The C. P. City library was the only library which
reported more than four areas in which citizens participated
in policy making. During the interviews it became evident
that there is indeed participation of citizens, but it is indirect; indirect in the sense that the citizen groups are, for
example: 1) multi-purpose staff unions which have some input into the procedures used for determining salaries and
promotions;[16] and 2) any group which wishes to make direct
petition to the library administration. While these are forms
of citizen participation, they do not represent formally organized and recognized groups with direct input into the total
decision-making process of the library.

Direct, non-traditional, citizen participation at the

C. P. City library is evidenced principally in two programs.
One, a Model Cities-funded program shows formally organized
citizen participation; the other, the library's storefront library
program, exhibits largely informal and intermittent citizen
participation.   Although the library reported in the questionnaire response that there were 30 storefront library advisory
groups, the interviews revealed that in actuality there were
no formal advisory groups, but rather that staff of the agencies in which book collections were placed had in some
cases advised their nearest branch librarian that books were
wanted and in many of the cases outlined the types of books
desired.

Citizen Participation in the Model Cities Library Project

The Model Cities library project was begun before the
Library Services and Construction Act-funded storefront library program.   The Model Cities project is small in scope,
but appears (there has been no formal evaluation of the project) to be having a large impact in terms of: 1) the heavy
use of the facility;[17] 2) the statement by the chairman of the
Model Cities Library Action Committee that the Committee
"hopes to be able to request funds for an additional service
outlet" of this type for the model neighborhood;[18] and 3) the
reference to the program by the press, including city-wide,
local and the Model Neighborhood papers, as "the most successful of all Model Cities' activities. "

Citizen participation with reference to the Model
Cities library facility has been for the most part advisory
in nature.   Although I made no attempt to determine what
strategy of citizen participation characterizes the total C. P.
City Model Cities program,[19] and thus cannot determine

whether the advisory mode is determined predominantly by
the general philosophy of the C. P. City Model Cities program or by the philosophy of the library staff; with regard
to the Library Action Committee, the citizen participation
activity is closest to being a strategy of organizational maintenance by using citizens as communications links between
planners and beneficiaries. [20] Although the project was initially proposed by the Citizens Library Committee, and
recommendations for sites, materials and staff members
were made by the Committee, the library staff has made all
final decisions.

In this incidence of citizen participation, neither party
was, or is now, contentious. The Library Committee proposed a project that is well within the confines of a traditional definition of library service; they requested that a credentialed librarian be in charge of operations; and they requested materials which are non-controversial.

During the interviews with the central library staff,
three staff members stated, with reference to the Model
Cities library project, that "the users don't use or check
out the books much. " Little enthusiasm was expressed by
the majority of staff interviewed about the success of the
project simply in terms of library visits. Except for two
members of the top-level administrative staff, none of the
persons interviewed mentioned citizen participation as a fact-
or in the success of the Model Cities Library project; five
professional staff members said that they did not know that
there was a Committee made up of neighborhood residents
which helped to direct the project.

It is difficult to assess in terms of power to what
degree citizens might be able to exercise their role in decision-making within the confines of the Model Cities library

project.   The Library Action Committee's one real potential
power is that funds for the project are Model Cities funds
and that without continued interest by the citizens, the library project might be discontinued.   It is equally difficult
to assess just how important the project is within the total
library program.   It is a small project and does not involve
much of the library's staff time or funds.   Perhaps because
the project is not considered particularly innovative and because it does operate smoothly and with some success, its
administrative characteristics are largely ignored.   There is
no evidence from the interviews or from written accounts of
the project's success that any of the library's other projects
are likely to be modeled after it, or even that it may lead
to the initiation of other similar projects.   Certainly, citizen
participation as perhaps a key facilitating factor in its success has not been identified.

The Model Cities library project affords the one example of structured non-traditional citizen participation at
the library.   All other cases are informal and intermittent.
Although it is well to remember that the board and top-level
administration of the library say that they plan to initiate
more formal channels of citizen participation through the development of branch library advisory groups and/or boards,
these plans are not now even being formulated.   There is
scant evidence, except for the subtle tone of two library
board members, that citizens will be active to any greater
degree in the proposed advisory groups and boards than they
are presently in the Model Cities project.   Again, it is clear
that citizen participation in the policy making process of C.
P. City library is considered to be primarily a public relations tool rather than a management technique.

Storefront Libraries

The library reported that its storefront libraries project involves citizen participation. The project is presently
receiving the library's greatest publicity effort (which in this
case is not translatable to interest or support). While library service offered to non-traditional publics outside of li-
brary-maintained facilities has developed a history in the library field (projects began in the early 1960's), C. P. City
library has only recently begun to reach out. It thus must
be the flush of newness which makes this project so note-
worthy to the library staff; it certainly is not because the
program is one of great importance to the total library program. (No attempts to redistribute library funds so as to
provide outreach programs without federal funds were reported.) As one staff member has written (as cited in an
unpublished paper by a master's degree student at a library
school in the C. P. City area):

> However, despite its administrative backing (in
> 1965) Project_____ was unable to get funded and
> no outreach program began until 1969 when the li-
> brary received its $25,000 grant from the Library
> Services and Construction Act, Title I.

The storefront libraries in C. P. City are in actuality simple collections of books placed in existing service
agencies throughout the city. These agencies requested that
the library place book collections at their facilities. It appears, for the most part, that the collections serve as a de-
vice for interior decoration or a means of adding a little
class to waiting areas. It is interesting to note that many
of the persons interviewed emphasized that when citizens
participate in library decision-making there is a great need
for professional and technical advice, but when a citizen par-

ticipation situation arose, the philosophy of "give 'em what
they want" took hold.

    In one of the storefronts which was visited, it was
necessary to go to a basement, remove several cases of
food and clothing which had been donated to the agency, and
then unbolt a door in order to see the book collection. It
was reported by two library staff members that this particular agency has recently received national recognition and is
now frequently visited by persons from all over the country.
The fact that this is such a blatant example of ineffectual library service was not mentioned by the librarians. (Of
course, in its present location it is highly unlikely that anyone would discover that it is there; still, one would think
that under the present circumstances the library staff would
engage in discussion with the agency staff and have the collection removed if it does not serve a purpose.) The librarians apparently feel that it serves a purpose simply because they are able to say that there is a library collection
at that agency. As one of the interviewed librarians said,
"Well, the past administrator of the agency asked for some
books, so we purchased some. The present administrator
is not so interested. " Evidently, neither are the responsible
librarians.

    To report this kind of situation as library outreach
entailing cooperative effort between librarians and citizens
is deceiving. Although it may be that not all the storefront
libraries developed in C. P. City are of such limited success, in the five collections I visited there was no one using
the collection and few materials were recorded as presently
circulating. The paper by the master's degree student cited
above reported the discovery of one successful storefront
collection. At this location an agency staff member asked

for and received training from the library and he makes use
of and maintains the book collection as an integral part of
his agency duties. 21

There is a distressing lack of purpose in the storefront libraries program. A few thousand dollars spread over
30 agencies, with continued funding uncertain, and professional staff whose interests do not center upon either the collections or their potential users, does not amount to pur-
poseful library service. The storefronts, like the branches,
are largely empty. As expressed by the branch librarians
in charge of the storefront collections who were interviewed,
the purpose of the storefronts is operationally rather than
goal-oriented; i. e. , storefronts bring book collections closer
to library users who are far away from branches, and they
will hopefully encourage people to come to their nearest
branch for additional material. The closest statement to a
goal expressed was: "Storefronts provide an opportunity to
develop a reading habit or to renew an interest in reading. "
Surely though, opportunity entails more than merely deposit-
ing collections of books around town. I am forced to wonder
what the staff of the C. P. City library has been considering
since library outreach programs began. Certainly they have
not been reading the evaluations of similar projects which
are readily available. 22

During the past several years some forms of citizen
participation in library operations have been taking place.
As is the case in most cities, the existence of at least one
branch of the library is largely attributable to the influence
of a neighborhood or community organization. The newest
branch of the C. P. City library is an example of this phenomenon. The community expressed their desire for a library and then the library took over. Perhaps it was in the

glitter of success and bustle of opening the library that the
citizen interest was lost. It evidently did not occur to the
library staff that the energies which created the library
would be useful in directing its programs and services.
There is no evidence that the profession has been able to
devise a model for successful branch library service; since
this is the case, to lose a source of possible intelligence for
discovering effective forms of library service, under the
name of professional prerogative, is both unimaginative and
unprofessional.

Information-Oriented Services

As has previously been mentioned, a minority of the
professional staff of the C. P. City library, but the majority
of its top-level administrative staff, are convinced that the
library should, must and will reorient its major service to
the general public--from the provision of books to the provision of community information reference and referral service. In essence, this service is being designed to provide
accurate information on where to obtain either help or more
detailed information about all services and activities available to city residents from any source. Again, as previously mentioned, a master file which will serve as the base for
this service has been under construction for the past year
and limited federal funds have been secured to begin pilot
operation in the near future. The long-range intent is to re-
produce the master file for each branch library and to have
branch library personnel supplement the file with local information. The supplemented file would contain information
such as lists of local residents who will, for example, super-
vise children after school hours; feed dogs while owners are

on vacation; teach quilting, etc. , as well as information on
local social service agencies.

The receptivity to this new service by the branch librarians interviewed is best described as either hesitant or
antagonistic. The reasons behind this less than enthusiastic
reception are basically two. First, the consensus of those
interviewed is that the majority of branch librarians do not
consider this kind of service a legitimate extension of the
library's reference function. They consider this work to be
"social work" or "that's the sort of thing the Mayor's Office
should be doing. " The second reason (which was cited by two
of the branch librarians, who felt that they could identify a
small number of staff who would concur) is that in order to
offer the service, knowledgeable staff, committed to maintaining, publicizing and encouraging its use through the local
area, must be secured. Only one person interviewed was
so bold as to say: "We can't push around books and information too in here!" One branch librarian stated that the
community information center model is "probably the direction the branch ought to take, " but showed great respect for
the enormity of such a transposition in branch library operations. He cited specifically the following problems: 1) staff
acceptance; 2) re-training; 3) file maintenance, and 4) com-
municating the change to community residents.

During the interviews, with the exception of one
branch librarian, no mention was made either of involving
existing citizen groups or of forming special citizen groups
to oversee or help direct the development of the community
information service. The assistant director, who states
that citizen participation is a vital source for information
and for aid in the management of library programs, and who
is largely responsible for initiating the information center

services program at the library, did not mention citizens in
any relationship to the service other than as recipients.

There was no indication given that the staff member
responsible for the compilation of the information service
master file had made an attempt to survey thoroughly the information sources presently available in the city in an attempt to coordinate, supplement or obtain cooperation in the
development of the service which is being designed. One
staff member mentioned a now defunct federally funded project which had had similar intents, but had proven unsuccess-
ful. No indication was given that the successes and failures
of this project had or would be investigated so as to provide
intelligence for the library's project. Knowledge of similar
activities being initiated by other libraries and city agencies
was found to be minimal. For example, the librarian in
charge of the information service had never heard of the
Model Cities Community Information Center of Philadelphia
which is partially funded by the Philadelphia Free Library
and has received national publicity both within and outside the
library profession.

The actual shift toward information-oriented services
at the C. P. City library is largely a matter of the top-
level administration's vision of the future. The amount and
source of funds, and the number of staff which form the base
for such a shift, do not provide convincing evidence that a
major reorientation of services will occur within the decade
of the 1970's. The capacity for reorientation of the majority
of the staff members who are to be utilized in delivering the
new service is reported as severely limited; this certainly
bodes ill for the success of the program.

<u>Conclusion</u>

The case study has revealed that what appeared, in terms of the survey analyses, to be a deviant case--i.e., a library which utilizes citizen groups in the policy making process to a considerable extent and additionally is characterized by a decentralized decision-making structure and information-oriented goal priorities--in actuality is a rather typical case, exhibiting minimal use of citizen group input, a relatively centralized decision-making structure, and traditionally-oriented goal priorities. Therefore, it seems necessary to add a further caution to the interpretation of the survey data given in the Appendix. It may be that despite the precautions taken to secure valid data, the questionnaire elicits <u>propensities to embrace</u> various patterns of citizen participation and also decision-making styles and orientations of service policies, rather than <u>actual incidents</u> of the characteristics. If the data are to be interpreted from this point of view, not only are incidents of these characteristics rare, but even a fruitful field for change in the direction of decentralized decision-making, citizen participation and information-oriented services is not in evidence.[23]

During the interviews it became clear that the major reason why the C. P. City library was characterized as a deviant case on the basis of the survey data is that the Assistant Director, the person who completed the questionnaire, desperately hopes, and in part actually perceives, that the C. P. City library is an institution of a different management and service nature than it, in reality, is. As the interviews probed more deeply into the situation at the library the discrepancy between perception and reality became increasingly clear. In terms of the six primary interview concerns it was discovered that:

1) There was only one citizen group which actually played a role in any part of the library's policy making process; this role was contained within a small project, and within the project appeared to be rather limited. This citizen group's chairman reported the group to be "relatively representative of the less alienated" portions of the community in terms of socially descriptive criteria. With reference to formal representation criteria, the committee chairman is directly elected by the service area constituents but some of the Library Action Committee members are chairman appointees.

2) The influence which the Library Action Committee appears to have is contained within the Model Cities project. The library staff members interviewed made no comments which indicated that the relative success of the Model Cities library program might be in part attributable to citizen involvement in the project or that the Library Action Committee might serve as a model for citizen participation in other library programs; neither, however, did the chairman of the Library Action Committee proffer such extrapolations. In relation to the extent of power which the Library Action Committee has, it is difficult to assess because of the lack of contention so far experienced between the Committee and the library staff; further, without an analysis of the Committee's general coalition capacities, it is difficult to know what levels of pressure they could bring to bear against the library.

3) With the clear exception of two library board members and, less clearly, two library staff members, none of the persons interviewed was able to verbalize a more than one-dimensional understanding of citizen participation objec-

tives and processes; i. e. , the complexities of the process
had not been perceived, or at least could not be verbalized
by the majority of the administration and staff.

4) The majority of those interviewed felt that citizen
participation at the C. P. City library either was (if they
believed citizen participation was indeed being practiced) or
should be principally a public relations technique.   Citizen
participation is considered to be a communications channel
functioning to allow the library's program messages to be
heard by key community individuals; only a few interviewees
mentioned that it could be a means by which the library
could be aided in devising what might possibly be more effective library administration and/or services.

5) The largest portion of those interviewed was not
able to express a general attitude toward citizen participation
in policy making processes because citizen participation had
not been previously contemplated.   The most typical response
from the interviewees was similar to: "Citizens must be
carefully instructed, if they are to participate in library decision-making, that there are great limits to their understanding of what library services are. "

6) None of the persons interviewed indicated that the
citizen participation which does now exist at the library had
had any type of effect on the library's management style or
orientation of service policies; further, with the exception of
the majority of the library board and a few of the top-level
administrative staff, none of the interviewees perceived that
citizen participation could have effects in these areas.

Despite this negative analysis of the present and probable near-future situation at the C. P. City library, at least
with reference to the development of a new style of leadership proposed by the library's top-level administration, this

could be an exemplary library.[24]   Perhaps, through this one
asset alone, the library may be able to extricate itself from
the morass of its minimal outreach programs and focus the
library's services in a more efficient and effective manner.[25]
Although leadership style alone is not enough to transform
an organization,[26] in this case, where the institution's goals
are poorly formulated, where the staff is largely operationally rather than goal-oriented, and where extra-institutional
forces exert great threats, a change-oriented, participative
and forceful management style is undoubtedly a key component of survival and growth.[27]

     Ralph Blasingame, in discussing the future of the ur-
ban main library, points out the differences between the
cities of the industrial revolution and post-industrial cities.
Of the industrial revolution cities he states:

> ... it seems possible to find directions for those
> libraries in community service of one kind or
> another....   In thinking of the potential for new
> courses of action, one must hope for: (1) new
> leadership less concerned with national norms than
> with local viability, (2) development of a series of
> goals, (3) development of measuring devices to es-
> tablish effective feedback systems, and (4) major
> overhaul of present administration styles.[28]

C. P. City is a city of the industrial revolution. The administration of its library appears to be trying to provide
change leadership. Yet, the top level administration at the
library must air the differences in goal perception which
exist among its members if they hope (as their majority professes) to change the library's priorities. The unstated but
clearly visible conflict prevents the library's leadership from
providing well-defined service goals which the majority of
the library staff and especially its professional staff need in
order to kindle vitality in their concern for the library's

programs. The conflict also militates against the library administration's capacity to take advantage of those aspects of the political environment of the city, e. g., its history of pressure politics through the use of active and influential special interest groups, which could help to shore up the library's crumbling credibility with the city administration.

It is not a foregone conclusion that the C. P. City library cannot serve its public; it is basically that the majority of the staff of the library does not appear either to know whether it does service a significant portion of its public, [29] or, most critically, even to care whether it does. These conclusions are evidenced principally by 1) the lack of knowledge on the part of the majority of the key professional staff of what services, programs and techniques have been utilized by other libraries and/or agencies offering library-type services; 2) the levels and sources of funds used by the library to provide non-traditional library services or even traditional services to non-traditional clienteles; and 3) the lack of continued involvement with and evaluation of the programs offered once they have been initiated.

Notes

1. He has an item veto which can only be overridden by majority council action.

2. He has consistently cut the library's budget beyond the point of simple containment to a level close to destruction of all but the central library's collection development and programs.

3. Until 1971, one of C. P. City's most influential and active citizens, a past member of the city council, was a library board member.

4. However, the severity of the city's financial ills, barring major shifts in the library's programs or in

state and federal aid to cities, will, perhaps in the next several years, overcome the past successes of the library lobby forces.

5. One professional staff member declared during the interview that "The amount of communication between the board and staff is inversely proportionate to the gravity of the situation."

6. It is interesting to note that many of those who have been deeply involved both operationally and analytically with citizen participation feel much the same as do these board members. For example, Alan A. Altshuler in his book, Community Control: The Black Demand for Participation in Large American Cities (New York: Pegasus, 1970), p. 56, quotes the scholar S. M. Miller as noting that "in the present atmosphere participation is probably necessary if many services are to continue to function at all."

7. For a recent survey analysis of public library administrators see Mary Lee Bundy and Paul Wasserman, The Public Library Administrator and His Situation (College Park: University of Maryland, School of Library and Information Services, June 1970).

8. One non-professional employee interviewed said that he did not care for this type of informal communication channel and that "the only effective communication to those on top is through the union" (This union represents the non-professional library staff. There is another union which represents the professional staff). Another employee stated that "the union isn't much interested in what the library does, just what it's like to work here." The majority of the interviewed library employees who have been with the library for at least five years stated that the style of management had changed with the new administration; they felt that there was now much more "receptive" administration. A small number of employees who had been with the library for more than five years stated that the style of management had not changed, i.e., there was always an atmosphere of active staff participation in the library. All of those who stated this opinion had administrative positions before the change in library directors. Those who indicated a change were then and, in some cases, are still in non-super-

visory roles.

9. In fact, these meetings have not been held regularly
    and they are not well attended by staff outside the
    central library; however, it is the intent of the as-
    sistant librarian to continue and further emphasize
    this channel of non-supervisory and non-professional
    staff participation. Many of those interviewed who
    were entitled to go to these meetings were asked
    whether they considered these meetings an effective
    way to encourage staff participation in policy making.
    Only one indicated that he thought that in essence the
    meetings were an attempt to decrease union effective-
    ness and really a means by which the administration
    sought to quell discontent. All others felt it was a
    sincere attempt by the administration to hear directly
    the concerns and ideas of non-supervisory and non-
    professional employees.

10. The concept of incrementalism was defined by Charles E.
    Lindblom and is discussed in many of his articles and
    books including The Policy Making Process (Englewood
    Cliffs, N.J.: Prentice-Hall, 1968). Lindblom pro-
    poses that all major shifts in public policy are slow
    and come in pieces which may eventually add up to
    fundamental change, although at the time change takes
    place it appears to be conventional rather than radical.

11. American Library Association. Public Library Associ-
    ation. A Strategy for Public Library Change: Pro-
    posed Public Library Goals Feasibility Study (Chicago:
    American Library Association, 1972), p. 26.

12. Robert C. Wood, "When Government Works," The Pub-
    lic Interest, No. 18 (Winter 1970), p. 49.

13. This opinion is corroborated in the Proposed Public Li-
    brary Goals--Feasibility Study, op. cit., p. 25.

14. The author is not privy to the conversations of the top-
    level staff among themselves and although they do
    realize that they do in fact have varying opinions on
    what the library's priorities should be, it appears
    that any conflict which strikes so close to the funda-
    mental purpose of the library has been avoided.

15. Larry Earl Bone, "Study in Renewal: A Library In

Search of Itself, " Library Journal, XCVII (March 1,
1972), pp. 844-847.

16. The perception of employee participation as constituting
a form of citizen participation was voiced by two top
level library staff members. It may be that this
conception of citizen participation as a management
style rather than a communications or public relations technique is an important area to analyze further.

17. During the six days in which the author visited C. P.
City this was the only place outside of the central library and one incident at a branch library in which
the author observed librarians interacting with library
users.

18. The Library Action Committee chairman is also a member of the larger Model Neighborhood Action Board
and clearly understands the difficulties involved in
getting any program recommendation even to the point
of being placed on an agenda for discussion; thus the
phrase, "to be able to. "

19. Citizen participation strategies are discussed in detail
in Chapter I.

20. See the typological presentation of the citizen participation process in Chapter I, pages 7-8. Specifically
the citizen participation activity in the Model Cities
library program most resembles I. A. 3. Negotiation.

21. It is interesting to note that several branch librarians
spoke of the often mentioned problem of Carnegie libraries, i. e. , a facility provided without support;
these same librarians failed to see the analogy with
the storefront collections: materials, but no service.

22. For example, Virgil A. Clift, A Study of Library Services for the Disadvantaged in Buffalo, Rochester and
Syracuse (New York: New York University School of
Education, Center for Field Research and School Services, 1969); and, Charlotte B. Winsor, A Study of
Four Library Programs for Disadvantaged Persons
(Albany: New York State Library, 1967). In addition, there are, of course, the many reports available in the popular literature of librarianship.

23. And, as Bundy and Wasserman point out "... even a
    disposition toward alternatives to the conventional
    scheme of things do [sic] not equate with a propensity
    to change things. " op. cit. , p. 69.

24. Bundy and Wasserman, Ibid. , state that in terms of the
    general administrator "... the evidence ... reveals an
    administrative class whose personal characteristics,
    attitudes of mind and value assumptions strongly mili-
    tate against the assumption of a change agent role. "

25. As Thomas W. Shaughnessy puts it: "Tokenism and the
    provision of symbolic services will no longer pass. "
    Cf. "The Emerging Environment of the Urban Main
    Library, " Library Trends, 20 (April 1972), p. 761.

26. For an explanation of this point of view see Charles
    Perrow, Organizational Analysis: A Sociological View
    (Belmont, California: Wadsworth, 1970); especially
    pp. 27-49.

27. At least such is the contention of the participatory
    management scholars, Cf. Likert, op. cit.

28. Ralph Blasingame, "Future of the Urban Main Library:
    I, " Library Trends, 20 (April 1972), p. 772.

29. Of course, evaluation techniques are not in abundance
    for library services as is evidenced by the present
    work of the Public Library Association's Measure-
    ment of Effectiveness Study, Cf. PLA Newsletter, 11,
    no. 1 (1972), p. 3; however, lack of effectiveness
    measures is not the basic problem at the C. P. City
    library. The professional staff whose responsibility
    includes evaluation of branch library and outreach
    services states simply that "there is no time for
    evaluation. " The problem really appears to be either
    (1) preferring not to know due to fear of failure or
    perhaps, (2) simple disinterest.

Chapter 4

CITIZEN PARTICIPATION IN PUBLIC LIBRARIES

In any of its forms or for any of its purposes, citizen participation through organized groups which represent[1] non-traditional[2] library clienteles has been conspicuously ignored in the literature of librarianship. With few exceptions, this statement holds true for all types of library literature: research reports, and descriptions of or prescriptions for practice. Reports of conferences and symposia dealing with library services and, most critically, with library service to the disadvantaged, fail to consider citizen participation in any manner.[3] The principal study which identifies areas for research in the urban public library field largely ignores administrative problems in general and citizen participation in particular as fruitful or even necessary research concerns.[4] In studies of specific library environments, only rarely and with little depth is consideration given to citizen groups as a source of input for the policy making process.[5] With but three principal exceptions, those library-related materials which do mention formal citizen participation do not treat the concept with sufficient clarity for the reader to understand either to what extent (i. e., with what formal authority) or for what purpose(s) input from citizen groups is recommended.[6]

The three items which do deal with citizen participa-

tion in any depth are quite different from each other.   Two
are reports of research investigations[7] and the other is a
recent article promoting a new design for public library service. [8] One of the research reports devotes a short chapter
to "A Philosophical Position on Community Control of the
Library. " The report notes that during interviews with
users and non-users from the population being served by
outreach programs, comments to the effect that "libraries
should be decentralized with the branches becoming more
autonomous"[9] comprised one of the four most mentioned
areas of concern.   On the basis of the findings from the research study (and undoubtedly, based too upon the personal
convictions of the authors), it was decided to include a
chapter in the report on community control as a form of
citizen participation.   Two statements are quoted below to
express the essence of the philosophical position forwarded:

> It is ... proposed that one approach that should
> be considered in an overall plan to provide library
> services for the urban disadvantaged is the use of
> community organization techniques to combat the
> debilitating effects of poverty through the develop-
> ment of library services. ... If the residents of
> a community have a central role in decision-mak-
> ing (not one that involves the mere patronizing
> tokenism of the appointment of a few safe minority
> group members to an establishment oriented li-
> brary board), a greater feeling of power to influ-
> ence and a more accurate reflection of the true
> wishes of the community can be achieved. [10]

> It is suggested here that if a man, a life-long
> resident of the ghetto, is able to point to a neigh-
> borhood library and say, 'We decided what kind
> of a library it should be, we decided where it
> should be built, we decided which programs it
> should provide and we made the recommendations
> about what kinds of people the librarians should
> be,' then he is more likely to use that library,

and urge his children to use it and to advertise it
to his neighbors. [11]

The Olson research differs from the Clift study in
that instead of offering a philosophical argument in favor of
citizen participation, it presents an explicit technique whereby any group--e.g., board members, professional experts
or a community organization, or for that matter, even a
single individual--can outline their perceptions of optimal library service and then, using the same technique, investigate
how closely their present library approaches the optimal service design they have outlined. The instrument could also,
of course, be utilized to design library service where no
service presently exists. Although the process and instrument designed by Olson has great value for stipulating library service priorities, it is constrained by its focus on,
and base in, presently offered library services. If[12] public
librarians hope to develop an understanding of what present
non-users may detail as priority service for a library/infor-
mation institution, a less technically worded and pre-defined
instrument would need to be devised; however, the Olson
instrument would be an excellent model from which to design
such an instrument.

The recent article cited above which deals directly
with citizen participation is by Dr. Mary Lee Bundy. Dr.
Bundy's proposal focuses upon the actions which she feels,
based upon her research and teaching experiences, must be
taken by the majority of urban public libraries (and for that
matter, the majority of all public libraries whose clientele
is sufficiently large and/or diversified to require branch
service) if these libraries are to be able to continue operating in their present physically decentralized form. One of
these actions is the active involvement of local residents in

the decision-making process of their branch libraries. A
selection of statements from the conclusion to her article
shows how directly related to the concerns of this study her
proposals are:

> The tight grip which central management have on
> public library systems would have to yield to trans-
> fer of authority to the local branches.

> ... community people must be brought into the li-
> brary system under conditions of an internal reor-
> ganization which recognizes community expertise
> in more than the present subservient roles ...

> ... libraries must be put into the hands of the
> communities to whom they rightfully belong. De-
> centralization--the establishment of representative
> community boards at the neighborhood branch
> level--is one way, provided they are not coopted
> through the selection process or manipulated once
> into being. 13

At this point it seems important to direct this study
to a number of specific, though largely unanswerable, questions. Since it appears quite evident, based upon: 1) the
survey and case study results reported herein; 2) evidence
gathered from the literature of librarianship;14 and 3) the
results of the Public Library Association's recent Proposed
Public Library Goals--Feasibility Study, 15 that citizen participation in library policy making is not an important concern of professional librarians, library administrators and/or
library educators, 16 one might well wonder whether citizen
participation is simply not an area with which the library
ought to be concerned; i. e. , citizen participation has little
relevance to the problems which face American public libraries; or, citizen participation is already being practiced
in American public libraries.

I suggest that this is indeed not the case, but rather

that the political history of the public library militates
against concern with citizen participation, except in terms of
library boards with middle-class members.[17] Notwithstanding the probable resistance to, if not abhorrence of, citizen
participation in the public library's policy making process
on the part of (probably) the majority of the profession,[18] I
further propose that non-traditional forms of citizen participation ought to be sought out in a variety of library environments.   This proposal is made because many in the profession concur with Genevieve Casey's succinct statement that
"... totally workable patterns of service have yet to be
found ... "[19]   Although it is doubtful that the public library
will disappear totally from our cities in the foreseeable future (barring major technological innovations in the communications field and financial innovations in public service delivery systems, that is),[20] still, unless urban branch libraries, many of which are experiencing a decline in use,[21]
restructure their services to fulfill some constituency-realized
community need, their continued existence is undoubtedly
marked and probably unjustified.

        Certainly some in the profession have sought to ad-
dress the problem of declining branch and overall library
use.   Reports of specialized services and programs abound
in the field, and some modicum of success has been met.
Collections more relevant to the interests of certain user
groups have been developed and programs using non-print
media which may be more easily accepted or assimilated by
some groups[22] have been initiated.   Still, success has not
been overwhelming.   Some in the profession call for a large-
scale, nationwide reorientation of library service from a
recreational/educational reading purpose to community information purposes--e. g. , the assistant director at the case

study library--but knowing just what sort of information is needed is highly problematical. [23]

Additionally, library educators have sought to address the problem of declining library use by "recruiting" into the profession Blacks, Mexican-Americans, Puerto-Ricans, etc., etc. Even the American Library Association has opened an office of minority recruitment. Results attributable to this avenue toward change are, of necessity, capable of analysis only in the not too immediate future; however, it appears that the majority of programs to recruit minorities are opened only to fundamentally middle-class individuals. In my conversations with faculty members from a large number of library schools the problem of recruiting "qualified" persons to play professional roles in city libraries, and especially in branch libraries, is often mentioned. The assumption made is always that indigenous community personalities who could communicate library policies to and from potential users are not qualified to be library school students; only rarely has it been suggested that perhaps the required qualifications are not appropriate to the role to be played. The recent demise of the Urban Information Specialist Project, an attempt to provide professional education and creditionals to, for want of a better word, "ghetto" residents, may[24] indicate that the profession is not willing to accept non-middle class persons into its domain. Other programs which emphasize training for community library service have not indicated that they are seeking non-middle class persons as students. [25]

In the light of the problems which are widely acknowledged to beset the public library, and the none too successful responses to the problems that have been made, it may be that citizen participation is an area in which the pro-

fession should experiment more fully and systematically.
Although there have been some experiments with citizen participation in public libraries, they have been, for the most
part, limited to organizational maintenance goals. For example, community residents are employed either to legiti-
mize library programs or simply to aid a small number of
local residents through employment.[26] For many years New
York City public libraries, especially Brooklyn's libraries,
have employed community liaison personnel to help bridge
the gap between the library's services and community residents who seem to shrink back in either dismay or disgust
from library activities. This kind of role is a type of citizen participation, but it is not a role in which organized
groups of community residents are given formal decision-
making authority; undoubtedly local personnel do provide
some intelligence for the policy making process, but they do
not, in this role, appreciably alter the decision-making system for a library. In fact, one must wonder how often
recommendations for policy change from community liaison
personnel are sought out by the library administration and/or
professional staff, and how often those recommendations
which are proffered are seriously considered. The credentials barrier,[27] the self-conscious professionalism of the library field, is probably a major barrier to this form of citizen participation and, further, evidence that citizen participation by means of staff supplement is an important factor
in increasing library use is not available.

As long ago as 1967 John Frantz said that libraries
must begin a

> selective decentralization of library policies and
> procedures to recognize and accommodate radical
> differences between specific neighborhoods. One

> of the first things I learned when I went to Brook-
> lyn was that there is no such place. Brooklyn is
> a collection of very discrete neighborhoods, each
> with very different population, economic, social,
> and racial characteristics and very different re-
> actions to, and needs for, education and libraries.[28]

But the fundamental questions are not raised by Frantz; e.g.,
1) what library policies and procedures ought to be decentralized? 2) by whom will they be identified? and 3) how will
decentralization be implemented?

In addressing the first question, the conceptual model
of decentralized metropolitan political structures proffered
by Oliver P. Williams is helpful.[29] Williams bases his
model upon sociospatial units derived from economic location theory and cultural ecology. Of key importance to
understanding sociospatial units--e.g., households, factories,
churches, clubs, etc.--is the hierarchy of values which these
units seek. Williams discriminates between functional life
style values (such as a configuration of school, church and
transportation for a household, or accessibility to a labor
force, transportation and supporting industries for a business) and system maintenance functions (such as utility net-
works and waste-disposal services) as major sources of
metropolitan politics. He also sees a special group of sys-
tem-maintenance-type functions which he calls central facilities. Included in this group are museums, stadiums and libraries, which are necessary to sustain and support city life
but which, he maintains, "Generally ... are not major
sources of political friction." The central argument of
Williams' article is that "sociospatial units resist integration of ... life style services, but accept ... integration of
system maintenance services."[30] Williams further strength-
ens his model by placing the various city service functions

upon a continuum rather than a dichotomy of life-style and
system maintenance, therefore allowing such functions as library service, outside of the central facility, to be placed
toward the life-style end of the continuum.   I contend that
branch libraries are a part of the life-style configuration
which various sociospatial units seek to control.   Since
neighborhood configurations are discrete, branch libraries in
a city ought also to be discrete.   But the question still un-
answered is: what parts of the library function in the city
ought to be decentralized?

    Again, it appears that William's model is useful.   Li-
brary functions themselves can be viewed in terms of the
life-style/system maintenance continuum.   System maintenance
functions, which often equate with economies of scale, such
as book ordering and processing and interlibrary loan, can
easily be integrated for an entire library system within a
city or larger area.   These library functions do not have
much impact upon any specific library's life-style value con-
tribution.   On the other hand, materials selection, program
and service development and, in many cases, both professional and non-professional staffing do not lend themselves
to centralized decision-making or integration because, if they
are to serve a function for a sociospatial unit, they most
probably must reflect the life-style configuration of values
which characterize that unit.   The character of policy decisions which are to be made for life-style functions and system maintenance functions are disparate.   It therefore seems
advisable, at the least, to experiment with decentralized
policy making for branch libraries.   Perhaps the most homo-
geneous approach, in terms of the library's history, would
be to institute a number of branch library boards.

    While it has been suggested that the functions of a library can be understood in terms of the system maintenance/ life-style continuum and that perhaps it is the life style functions that best lend themselves to areas of decentralized decision-making, as Williams and others point out, in any specific environment even system maintenance functions can take on a highly politicized character. Therefore, branch library boards probably ought to be highly autonomous in defining the parameters of their decision-making authority.

It seems appropriate at this point to make it clear that the purpose of this chapter does not include defining an optimal form of citizen participation in library decision-making processes, but is rather to suggest some of the factors which seem of importance when citizen participation techniques are employed. While, to some in the profession, it may be shameful that libraries have not been more attuned to the pregnant atmosphere of decentralization and citizen participation in many cities, by arriving late library administrators may be able to avoid some of the difficulties, diseconomies, and ineffectiveness suffered by other fields, e. g., schools and welfare agencies, which have attempted to employ citizen participation techniques.

Much of the material in Chapter 1 dealt with the many purposes for which citizen participation techniques can be employed. Two considerations are raised again here in order to highlight the many dimensions of citizen participation and the importance of entering into any of its forms with an understanding of its elusive qualities and complexities.

One of the most perplexing dimensions of citizen participation is representation. As was discussed in Chapter 2, representativeness of a group's members can be analyzed and/or determined on the basis of their formal or socially descriptive representation characteristics. Peterson[31] also

details a dimension of "substantive representation" which
takes into account the actions of representatives in terms of
both their influence (Who will listen to what the representative says?) and interest orientation (Are the representative's
interests in accord with the constituent's?). Undoubtedly,
persons who are substantively representative of community
interests are those who would best be sought out as a group's
representatives; however, identifying these people is highly
problematical. In actual citizen participation situations,
three criteria have most commonly been used in determining
who shall be a representative. These criteria are: residence, income level and ethnicity. [32] Occasionally, one dimension of this trichotomy becomes of the highest priority
in a given situation, but most often citizen groups represent
some mix of these criteria. This short discussion of representation is offered only to highlight some of the difficulties in finding representative citizens once it has been determined to elect or appoint a group such as a branch library board.

The second consideration to be raised again is perhaps the most important aspect of citizen participation:
namely, the purpose/goal/objective/reason why citizen participation is undertaken. As discussed in Chapter 1, citizen
participation can be described in terms of two basic goals:
goals concerned primarily with its impact on the citizen
participators themselves (i. e. , individual goals) and goals
concerned with its impact on an institution's operations (i. e. ,
organizational goals). Most analyses of citizen participation
situations state that these goals rarely appear in isolation;
rather both are sought, but with varying degrees of concen-
tration on one or the other type of goal.

Davis and Dolbeare, in their study of the Selective

Service System, which includes an analysis of local selective
service board characteristics and operations, concur with
other researchers concerned with citizen participation about
the duality of goal seeking. [36]   They offer an additional proposal: i. e., as the balance between the two types of goals
converge (taking into consideration who the participators are
and the degree of power available to the participants), the
greater is the likelihood that citizen participation will be effective for both the citizens and the organization.

The balance of citizen participation goals in the public library environment at this time appears to be heavily
weighted towards organizational goals.   Elites, or at least
unrepresentative groups of citizens, are the usual library
board members, and they tend to play, for the most part,
moderately powerful policy making roles. [34]   This configuration of representation and power emphasizes organizational
goals according to Davis and Dolbeare:

> Participation by elites or unrepresentative groups
> of citizens suggests priority for organizational
> goals under any conditions: if there is little or
> no participation in policy making, the implication
> is that the local elite is being used to gain consent
> or to more effectively implement the organization's
> goals; if there is policy involvement, it is likely
> to be on a quid pro quo basis, in which the organi-
> zation confers authority on the local elites in order
> to get its tasks accomplished, avoids challenging
> them on the way in which they do the job, and in
> return secures support from them for the basic
> task. [35]

In order to strike a "better" balance between organizational and individual goals of citizen participation in the
library environment, library boards and/or branch library
boards representative of either the general public or of proposed clientele group members who have high levels of policy

making power in terms of both policy substance and application should be developed. This change of representativeness and power in library boards does not constitute abrogation of either professional expertise or organizational maintenance goals; rather, it represents a possible avenue for change and perhaps survival for the public library, for it may be that through citizen participation of this type a larger, more general, goal may be pursued. This general goal could have societal impact because it may, at the same time, provide 1) the intelligence for making better policy decisions for the library, because citizens may know more about the details of educational and informational problems in their communities than their librarians, or simply because the policy decisions they make are correct insofar as they solve resident problems and/or meet their preferences; and 2) the beginning of public confidence in the library from a group who have long been alienated from the institution.

Davis and Dolbeare conclude from their study that although there are always individual situation characteristics which intervene, in general, citizen participation has its best chance for success in organizations

> ... whose missions are general in character, admitting of local variations, and which further involve public behavioral consequences inspirable through participation. 36

On all three of these organizational attributes the institution of the public library seems to provide a receptive field. Surely, the lack of goal specificity has long been acknowledged throughout the field, and despite the history of public library standards, local variations in library services are increasingly being tolerated and even planned. Further, the general mission of the library has always been to provide an avenue through which an individual, either for himself or for his fellow man, can seek enlightenment or improvement. It would seem, therefore, that the profession should take steps to right the imbalance between individual and organization goals in its practice of citizen participation, thereby, perhaps, approaching more closely its avowed institutional goals. Citizen participation is not offered as a panacea for the problems besetting library service. In fact, based upon the results of citizen participation practice in the past decade, an additional perplexing set of problems including, perhaps, higher costs and surely more complex governmental relations would arise; however, it would increase the involvement of the library within community life and might promote improved delivery of library and/or information systems.

Although theoretically the library may provide a receptive ground for the practice of citizen participation, the literature reporting relevant library operations and research, the results of my survey and case study, and the "sense" of the profession gleaned from personal conversations with public library administrators and staff as well as library educators, come together to form a rather guarded view of the capacity of the library to restructure its decision-making style by means of the active participation of citizen groups representative of persons other than its traditional clientele. The survey data illustrates that the responding libraries tend to be highly centralized in their decision-making style (only 29 percent of the libraries are classified as participative) and that the majority of the top level administrators appear to have less than receptive attitudes towards the concept and/or practice of citizen participation (only 29 percent are classified as receptive). Further, 72 percent of the libraries imply that there are no opportunities available for citizen

participation in library policy making, and where citizen input is accepted the average percent of participation across
the ten decision-making areas listed is only six percent.
The case study reveals that even where a library administration professes an inclination towards the utilization of citizen
group intelligence, the translation of that inclination into reality is problematical.   However, despite the apparently
limited responsiveness of the field, it is felt that further research and the initiation of pilot projects utilizing citizen
participation can fruitfully be undertaken.   Recommendations
for such action are presented in the following Chapter.

Notes

1.   In terms of either or both socially descriptive and for-
     mal representation criteria as discussed in Chapter 2.

2.   In terms of both: 1) present library user groups not
     usually represented on library boards, e. g., stu-
     dents; and 2) present non-user groups, e. g., medium
     to low income blacks.

3.   For example, New York (State) Library. Extension Di-
     vision. Proceedings of a Conference on Library Par-
     ticipation in Antipoverty Programs, Thayer Hotel,
     Westpoint, February 7-9, 1966 (Albany: 1966); and,
     Emory University. Division of Librarianship. Pub-
     lic Library Services to the Disadvantaged: Proceed-
     ings of an Institute, December 7-8, 1969 (Atlanta:
     1969). A list of examples could be extended to in-
     clude virtually all works on library service in urban
     areas and in library service to the disadvantaged with
     but two exceptions which will be cited below.

4.   Henry Voos. Information Needs in Urban Areas (New
     Brunswick, N. J.: Rutgers University Press, 1969).
     And further, in one of the more recent articles deal-
     ing with administration and serving the disadvantaged
     --Cf. Marie A. Davis, "Serving the Disadvantaged
     from the Administrative Viewpoint," Library Trends,
     XX (October 1971), pp. 382-391--there is but one

paragraph dealing with citizen participation and it is focused on the usual community relations level.

5. For example, Lowell Martin in his Library Response to Urban Change: A Study of the Chicago Public Library (Chicago: American Library Association, 1969) mentions only a broad-based "friends of the library" type group, i. e., "Citizens for the Chicago Public Library, " as a recommendation. (Cf. p. 211).   Nowhere in the study are branch library boards or advisory groups advocated or even mentioned.   The suggestion offered which relates most closely to citizen participation is his statement that: "Effective methods for reaching people in the disorganized sections of the city are not known.   But, certain principles are clear enough ... close planning and working relationships with local residents is necessary. " (Cf. p. 212.)

6. For example, Judith Guthman's Metropolitan Libraries: The Challenge and the Promise (Chicago: American Library Association, 1969) states only "the necessity of consulting with the people who are potential users. " (Cf. p. 25).

7. Virgil A. Clift. A Study of Library Services for the Disadvantaged in Buffalo, Rochester and Syracuse (Albany: New York University, School of Education, Center for Field Research and School Services, 1969); and Edwin E. Olson, Survey of the User Service Policies in Indiana Libraries and Information Centers (Indiana Library Studies, Report 10, 1970.   ERIC ED044139.)

8. Mary Lee Bundy. "Urban Information and Public Libraries: A Design for Service, " Library Journal, XCVII (January 15, 1972), pp. 161-169.

9. Clift, op. cit., p. 41.

10. Ibid., p. 50.

11. Ibid., p. 51.

12. The Olson report evidence "suggests" that user relations is not an area of priority concern in the public libraries of Indiana.

13. Bundy, op. cit., p. 169.

14. With the exceptions noted in this chapter, plus such
     rare examples of concern with representation, e.g.,
     appointing high school students to a few library
     boards, and true wide-spread community involvement
     as Terre Haute, Indiana experienced in the Vigo
     County Public Library's railroad car library incident.

15. American Library Association. Public Library Asso-
     ciation. A Strategy for Public Library Change: Pro-
     posed Public Library Goals--Feasibility Study, Allie
     Beth Martin, project coordinator (Chicago, 1972).

16. The notable exception here is Ralph Blasingame as
     cited in the conclusion to Chapter 3 of this study.

17. See Oliver Garceau, The Public Library in the Politi-
     cal Process (New York: Columbia University Press,
     1949); and Mary Lee Bundy and Paul Wasserman,
     The Public Library Administrator and His Situation
     (College Park: University of Maryland, School of
     Library and Information Sciences, June 1970).

18. Reticence to citizen participation does, after all, have
     some base, especially in relation to intellectual free-
     dom concerns. Not a few librarians have been sore-
     ly tested by various groups campaigning for the re-
     moval of materials from library collections.

19. Cited in Margaret E. Monroe, "Education in Librarian-
     ship for Serving the Disadvantaged," Library Trends,
     20 (April 1972), p. 456.

20. At the least, the central or main library would remain,
     with deposit collections and services to the handicap-
     ped, aged and incarcerated continuing as forms of
     service decentralization.

21. Although a survey of public libraries reported in Doug-
     las M. Knight and E. Shepley Nourse, eds., Li-
     braries at Large (New York: Bowker, 1969) reports
     that of 129 libraries of various sizes, 68 reported
     increased use of branches and only 15 reported de-
     creased use of branches (Cf. p. 24), specific studies
     such as Martin, op. cit., p. 77, report "the fall-off
     in branches was steady during and after World War

II.   A partial recovery occurred during the 1950's.
Circulation in the branches held fairly even in the
first years of the present decade, but fell again during 1965, 1966 and 1967." Book circulation in general in Chicago between 1938 and 1968 had fallen from
over 12 million to around 9 and 1/3 million (Cf. p.
77), while the population in the past 20 years has remained relatively stable (Cf. p. 1). Charles S. Benson and Peter B. Lund in their study, Neighborhood
Distribution of Local Public Services (Berkeley: University of California, Institute of Governmental
Studies, 1969), clearly demonstrate that in neighbor-
hoods which contain a majority of non-middle class
households, the consumption of library services is
low.

22.   A series of research studies done by the Michigan
State University Department of Communications, under
the direction of Bradley S. Greenberg, which focus
upon communication among the urban poor, are highly applicable to the field of multi-media library services.

23.   The identification of just what are the informational
needs of urban dwellers remains a field of many
questions and few answers. The Voos study, op. cit.
is one of the earliest attempts to suggest that research is sorely needed in this area. Present projects, such as the Model Cities Community Information Center in Philadelphia, are beginning to accumu-
late sufficient data upon which to judge what are the
information needs of informationally deprived urban
residents. A study of information needs in Baltimore
is presently underway by Westat Research Inc. of
Rockville, Maryland for the U.S. Office of Education
and Baltimore's Regional Planning Council.

24.   The circumstances surrounding the lack of renewed
funding for the project are highly complex.

25.   Although I believed that one library school was presently attempting to formulate a total school curriculum
to train a different breed of librarian (The Graduate
Library School at the University of South Carolina
was reported to be designing a curriculum to train
librarians for "the American library's new role as a
community information center" by Library Journal,

XCVI, December 1, 1971, p. 3934), in a discussion
with one of the school's faculty members I learned
that this was an inaccurate report; however, faculty
at the University of Toledo report that they are attempting to develop a program which will require "non-
traditional" students in order to realize its goals.

26. For further discussion of types of citizen participation,
     see Chapter 1, pp. 5-12.

27. See S. M. Miller, Breaking the Credentials Barrier
     (New York: The Ford Foundation, 1967). (SR/26).

28. Guthman, op. cit., p. 31.

29. Oliver P. Williams, "Life Style Values and Political
     Decentralization in Metropolitan Areas," Southwestern
     Social Science Quarterly, XLVIII (December, 1967),
     pp. 299-310.

30. Ibid., p. 305.

31. Paul E. Peterson, "Forms of Representation: Partici-
     pation of the Poor in the Community Action Program,"
     American Political Science Review, LXIV (June,
     1970), pp. 491-507.

32. Ralph M. Kramer, Participation of the Poor (Engle-
     wood Cliffs, N.J.: Prentice-Hall, 1969), p. 193.

33. James W. Davis, Jr. and Kenneth M. Dolbeare, Little
     Groups of Neighbors: The Selective Service System
     (Chicago: Markham, 1968), pp. 220-240.

34. Evidence supporting this contention can be found in
     Chapter 2, pp. 36-40 and 43-51.

35. Davis and Dolbeare, op. cit., p. 227.

36. Ibid., p. 236.

Chapter 5

RECOMMENDATIONS FOR RESEARCH AND PILOT PROJECTS

The Proposed Public Library Goals--Feasibility Study
states that "prototypes and application in real life through
demonstration are necessary steps in the strategy for public
library change. "[1] I agree with this recommendation of the
Feasibility Study. Experimentation with different forms of
citizen participation in the policy making process of libraries
lends itself to the demonstration technique.

The field of potential sites for demonstration projects
is great. Although some libraries may be constrained by
city ordinance or state law from granting formal decision-
making powers to local boards, there are no constraints on
obtaining and acting upon "advice" offered from citizen
groups. Several forms of citizen participation could be
tried in various settings. The projects might include cases
which emphasize organizational goals such as the development of improved service delivery systems; other projects
might emphasize individual goals such as increased feelings
of corporate efficacy or of personal self-reliance; and in
other cases the projects might concentrate on system change
goals such as impacting existing library power structures.

I am aware of one library which could provide base
intelligence for a series of similar demonstration projects.
The balance between organization and individual citizen par-

ticipation goals here appears to be well struck. The Langston Hughes Community Library and Cultural Center of Corona, Queens, New York[2] is a community controlled library. For the most part the library appears to have focused upon organizational/system change goals by means of impacting the existing power structure within the Queens Borough Public Library system.

The Langston Hughes Library was brought into being almost solely through the pressures exerted by an independent citizen group, the Corona-East Elmhurst Library Action Committee. Over a period of a decade this group pressured and finally gained support from the Queens Borough Public Library when federal funds for urban library extension became available. The Hughes library publicly announced a comprehensive plan in August 1968 and was formally dedicated in April 1969. It has been financed since opening through Library Services and Construction Act, Title I, funds granted to the Queens Borough Public Library.

The Library Action Committee has retained its independent character. It meets monthly along with a library executive board which include a Queens Borough Public Library liaison person. The executive board and the Library Action Committee direct the development of the library's services and programs. Indeed, this is a community-directed or -controlled library; it was planned by community residents and its location and premises where chosen and secured by community residents. At the dedication ceremony, Harold Tucker, the Queens Borough Public Library director, related:

> The first thing you told us is that you want the Center in a building of its own. Our search did not bring up anything very satisfactory. Then you

> said you wanted this building. When we pointed
> out that it was occupied by an active business that
> did not want to give it up, you undertook to get
> the building released by the business, and the land-
> lord to agree to a lease. In the process you sure
> taught us a lot. [3]

The staff was selected by and is made up of community residents who are not professional librarians. The staff is
backed up by the Queens Borough Public Library by one professional librarian who provides technical/professional assistance.

The Langston Hughes Library was initially reported
to be a success; it remains a success according to those interviewed and according to the activities taking place on the
day of my visit. On the day of the visit books and information files were in heavy use. There were people in the library participating in the following types of programs:
1) reading improvement; 2) reading instruction; 3) tutoring
for civil service job examinations; 4) school counselors
meeting with mothers who would otherwise have to travel
long distances via uncertain public transportation in order
to have conferences at the schools where their children are
bused; and 5) teenagers helping to paint the recently re-
modeled second floor of the building which was acquired in
order to provide space for the burgeoning number of persons
utilizing the library.

At the dedication ceremony, Mr. Tucker opened his
remarks with: "There is nothing like the Langston Hughes
Library-Information-Cultural Center any place, anywhere!"[4]
To my knowledge, Mr. Tucker was then and remains right.
There are no other community controlled libraries; when
one stops to realize just how vital library service, in terms
of reading, information and education programs, is to the

Corona/East Elmhurst community of 30,000 low-income blacks and Puerto-Ricans, one wonders whether citizen participation may perhaps be a key factor in the library's vitality. It is difficult to assess to what extent citizen participation in the form of community control plays a role in the success of the library (success measured simply in terms of library visits and staff attitude), but at this time of declining branch library use and after the minimal and short-lived successes of many branch library programs, it seems apparent that librarians should look toward factors besides relevant content and media modes of materials and programs as important factors in creating demands for library services. Librarians may find that decision-making methods are an important factor in promoting branch library use. Demonstration sites should be found and experimentation with citizen control and other forms of citizen participation should be undertaken with, of course, the full understanding on the part of the citizen participators that they are taking part in library decision-making demonstration projects, not simply being taken.

In the area of research, it would seem useful to explore further the relationship between participative internal decision-making structure and the utilization of citizen participation in library policy making, despite the implications of such work as that of C. J. Lammers, who contends that internal and external forms of participation do not correlate in formal organizations.[5] A number of the libraries included in the survey portion of this study which reported participative internal decision-making structures could be investigated further, most fruitfully through the administration of structured interviews during site visits, in order to reveal possible structural and attitudinal factors within the library which bear upon the decision-making process. Also, constraint and opportunity factors operating in the external domain of these libraries could also be investigated. Such factors as the incidence and outcomes of citizen participation in decision-making for other service organizations in the city, the character of the city political structure, and the power coalition capabilities of citizen groups should be considered.

Another area of exploratory research could be the in-depth investigation of libraries such as Langston Hughes, Buffalo and Erie County, New York, Carnegie Library of Pittsburgh and Terre Haute, Indiana where branch library boards or other forms of citizen participation are presently being practiced.

A combination of pilot projects and research studies should complement one another and could produce a body of literature articulating the forms of citizen participation which are most likely to be fruitful if used in the formulation of public library policies.

Notes

1.   American Library Association.   Public Library Asso-
     ciation.   A Strategy for Public Library Change: Pro-
     posed Public Library Goals--Feasibility Study, Allie
     Beth Martin, project coordinator (Chicago, 1972),
     p. 52.

2.   I visited the Langston Hughes Library in October, 1971.
     Information reported here is taken from brochures
     made available by the library and from interviews
     with two community workers at the library; one of
     these workers has been active in obtaining the library
     over the past 13 years and is a member of the execu-
     tive board of the Library Action Committee.

3.   Langston Hughes Community Library and Cultural Cen-
      ter, Dedication Brochure (Corona, New York: April
      1969).

4.   Ibid.

5.   C. J. Lammers, "Power and Participation in Decision-
      making in Formal Organization," American Journal
      of Sociology, LXXIII (September, 1967), pp. 201-216.

Appendix A

STUDY DESIGN

Purpose of the Study

Taking its impetus from the keen interest in forms
of participatory management presently being shown in many
societal arenas, this study attempts to investigate the extent
to which forms of participatory management, particularly
forms of citizen participation, have impacted the institution
of the American public library. More specifically, the
study is undertaken in order to describe the forms in which
citizen participation takes place in library decision-making
processes; and further, to investigate whether citizen participation in the policy-making process effects the goals of library service programs.

Methodological Development

Although the case study method is best suited to explore the complex nature of the processes being studied,
because information on decision-making structure, citizen
participation and service policy priorities is minimal, it
was deemed necessary to undertake a preliminary survey.
Despite the many severe problems that often arise with a
mail questionnaire, this technique appeared to be the best-
suited method from both time and cost standpoints.

145

The questionnaire designed to collect data on decision-making structure, citizen participation and service goals was developed over a period of several months. It utilized major inputs from several sources, [1] and was pretested prior to final dissemination to a national sample of public libraries.

Sample

The sample was drawn from Table 4 of Statistics of Public Libraries Serving Areas with at Least 25,000 Inhabitants, [2] amended, to provide data for Georgia's public libraries as Georgia did not respond to the Office of Education survey. This sampling source provides data for 1,172 libraries, which is only 17 percent of the total 1968 population of public libraries (6,922); however, the frame does include 770 (60 percent) of the 1,289 public libraries with branches and 4,362 (90 percent) of the 4,855 branch libraries existing in 1971. [3]

Based upon a presample analysis it was decided that the sample could profitably be stratified by number of branches into five categories: 1) no branches; 2) 1-2 branches; 3) 3-8 branches; 4) 9-24 branches; and 5) 25 and more branches. An optimum allocation sample for each of the strata with branches was taken. In drawing the samples, the BMD 101 descriptive analysis program was run on stratum and aggregate data in order to compute standard deviations necessary to determine sample sizes.

Table 32 illustrates the sample sizes as they were constructed for this study. The choice of specific libraries for the sample was made through use of a standard random number table.

TABLE 32:   SAMPLE SIZE

Stratum	Number of Branches	Number of Libraries	Sample Sizes	Sampling Rate
1	0	402	57	14. 2%
2	1-2	310	57	18. 4
3	3-8	324	77	23. 8
4	9-24	115	42	36. 5
5	25-91	21	21	100. 0
		1172	254	

Reliability/Validity-Analyses

During the course of the study, two attempts were made to establish the validity and reliability of the data obtained by the questionnaire.   The purpose of conducting these tests was to determine the degree of confidence which could be placed on the study findings; i.e., these tests would indicate the margin of error in the data resulting from such problems as the interpretation of questions by respondents.

For the reliability test, ten libraries, two from each strata, were sent duplicate questionnaires in order to determine whether the questions could elicit the same response at two points of time.   Seven of the ten libraries completed the duplicate questionnaire.   A comparison of the responses of the libraries indicated that some of the questions were answered differently on the two occasions; however, in the most important categories for final data analyses no variance was observed.   The reliability rate for the questionnaire was calculated as 85. 7%.[4]   In order to make a validity test, a sample of five libraries (one from each stratum) was taken.   The test was undertaken in an attempt to determine whether the investigator could be certain the questions yielded the desired information about the decision-making structure, citizen participation pattern and library service

goals of the libraries sampled. The validity test was made
by means of a telephone interview and no significant variance in responses was obtained, although slight variability
was observed.

The analysis of the 12 questionnaires from the reliability and validity tests indicate that the average reproducibility index of a questionnaire is about 87.3%. [5]

Data Collection and Processing

All libraries in the sample received a letter explain-
ing the study, a questionnaire and a stamped, self-addressed
envelope for mailing the questionnaire to the author. Those
libraries which did not respond within four days after the
requested return date were sent a follow-up letter.

As the questionnaires were received, they were
edited, coded, verified, key punched and reverified. The
error rate due to coding and punching errors was calculated
to be in the vicinity of one percent.

The response rate of usable questionnaires was 52
percent. Rates of response varied from a low of 44.3 percent for libraries with 1-2 branches to a high of 67.4 percent for libraries with 9-24 branches.

Response Bias

When evaluating any survey one critical area of concern is possible bias due to omission from the survey of
those cases which did not respond. The number of libraries
included in the non-response bias analysis was kept small
due to the cost involved; however, it was felt that 15 cases
(15 percent of non-respondents) would be large enough to un-
cover an indication of bias.

Telephone interviews were conducted with personnel at the 15 libraries. The data collected from the non-responding libraries were coded and compared with the average mean scores of those of the respondents. Data for the comparisons were developed by computing confidence intervals based on the variance in the scores and using the Students t test at the 95% confidence level. No significant differences were revealed between the pairs of mean scores. Therefore, non-respondents are assumed not to have biased the findings of the survey.

Notes

1. Morris Hamburg and others, A Systems Analysis of the Library and Information Science Statistical Data System: The Research Investigation (Philadelphia: University of Pennsylvania, June, 1970); Rensis Likert, The Human Organization: Its Management and Value (New York: McGraw-Hill, 1967); and Edwin E. Olson, Inter-library Cooperation (Washington, D.C.: U.S. Office of Education, Bureau of Research, 1970) ED 046 421.

2. U.S. Office of Education. Library Services Branch. Statistics for Libraries Serving at Least 25,000 Inhabitants (Washington, D.C.: 1968), pp. 11-23.

3. Bowker Annual of Library and Book Trade Information, 1971 (New York: Bowker, 1971), p. 49.

4. Calculation: 1 change in 7; total response to question 26, 110; $1 - ((1/7)/110) = 1 - (15.71/110) = 85.72$.

5. Coefficient of Reproducibility =
    $$1 - \frac{(\text{No. of items with variability})}{\text{Total number of items}}$$

Appendix B

Instructions

1. Before answering a question, please read all possible answers.

2. Please keep in mind the entire organization of the library as you answer the questions; that is, if the library has branches, think in terms of the central library and all of the branches. (For library systems, consider member libraries as branches.) If the library has no branches, think in terms of the various departments or administrative units within the library.

3. Please enclose any available documents that will explain in greater detail the answers given.

****

I. LIBRARY STRUCTURE:

A. Branches

1. How many branches does the library have? _____.

B. Other Outlets

2. Does the library have bookmobiles?

☐ No   ☐ Yes
How many bookmobile stops are there? _____.
Are some bookmobiles administered directly from branch libraries?

☐ No   ☐ Yes

3. Does the library have deposit stations?

☐ No   ☐ Yes
How many? _____.
Are some deposit stations administered directly from branch libraries?

☐ No   ☐ Yes

C. Professional Staff

4. How many professional positions does the library have? _____.

5. How many professionals work outside of the main library building? _____.

150

D. General

   6. Circle the letter of the diagram that best illustrates how major policy
      decisions are made in the library; i.e., show the direction of decision
      making flow.

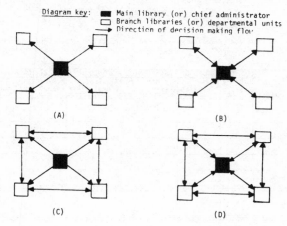

Diagram key: ■ Main library (or) chief administrator
                  □ Branch libraries (or) departmental units
                  → Direction of decision making flow

(A)   (B)

(C)   (D)

   (E) If you prefer, draw your own diagram:

II. POLICY MAKING:

  A. Staff Involvement

    7. To what extent are professional staff involved in the policy making process?

       ☐ Fully involved
       ☐ Often consulted, but not ordinarily involved in the actual policy
         making process
       ☐ Occasionally consulted, but rarely involved in actual decisions
       ☐ Never involved
       ☐ Don't know

8. To what extent are <u>non-professional</u> staff involved in the policy making process?

☐ Fully involved
☐ Often consulted, but not ordinarily involved in the actual policy making process
☐ Occasionally consulted, but rarely involved in actual decisions
☐ Never involved
☐ Don't know

9. For each decision making area listed below, check EACH category of participants that is <u>actively</u> involved in the decision making process.

DECISION MAKING AREAS	CATEGORIES OF PARTICIPANTS INVOLVED IN THE DECISION MAKING PROCESS						
	Library Board	Head Librarian	Key Administrative Staff	All Professional Staff	Non-professional Staff	Citizen Groups	Other (Specify)
PERSONNEL: a. selection of head librarian							
b. selection of professionals							
c. selection of non-professionals							
d. determining salaries							
e. determining promotions							
BUDGET: f. preparation of budget							
MATERIALS: g. selection of materials							
PROGRAMS: h. determining types of programs to be offered							
FACILITIES: i. determining building design							
j. site selection							

B. <u>Library Board</u>

10. Is there some type of library board associated with the library?

☐ Yes   ☐ No
How is the library governed?_____
_____
_____(Skip to Q.13).

11. In what way is the library board constituted?

☐ Appointed primarily by a private library association or group
☐ Appointed primarily by head librarian
☐ Appointed primarily by the city manager or mayor
☐ Appointed primarily by the city council or commission
☐ Elected from each school district
☐ Elected from each electoral district
☐ Elected at large
☐ Other (explain)_____.

12. Describe each library board member on the outline below. (If necessary, append an additional sheet.)

Member No.	Occupation		Race	Sex	Age (To nearest decade, eg. 40)	No. of years on board
	Where Employed	Title of Position				
1.						
2.						
3.						
4.						
5.						
6.						
7.						
8.						
9.						
10.						
11.						
12.						

C. Friends of the Library

13. Is there a Friends of the Library associated with the library?

☐ Yes   ☐ No
                 (Skip to
                  Q. 15)

14. Describe the leadership of the Friends of the Library on the outline below.

Member No.	Occupation		Race	Sex	Age (To nearest decade, eg., 40)	No. of years a Friend
	Where Employed	Title of Position				
1.						
2.						
3.						
4.						
5.						
6.						
7.						
8.						
9.						
10.						
11.						
12.						

D. Underline Other Advisory Groups

15. Does any branch have a library board or advisory group of its own?

☐ No   ☐ Yes
         How many branches have such groups? _____ .

16. Within the past year has any citizen group (other than the Library Board, Friends of the Library or other groups whose major orientation is toward the library) attempted to influence either library policy or administrative decisions?

☐ No   ☐ Yes
         Identify group(s) by name_____
         _____
         _____

III. CITIZEN PARTICIPATION:

Please respond to the following set of statements from your personal point of view.

		AGREE STRONGLY	AGREE	NO OPINION	DISAGREE	DISAGREE STRONGLY
17.	People have a clear idea of the types of services the public library offers.					
18.	Library effectiveness could be improved through greater communication with those its service is intended to benefit.					
19.	Increased citizen participation in library policy making causes more problems than its worth.					
20.	Citizen participation must NEVER enter into the area of administration.					
21.	Special boards (or other mechanisms) should be provided through which citizens may express their opinions regarding public services.					
22.	A significant number of citizens are motivated to participate in library policy making.					
23.	Library effectiveness could be improved through more active participation of citizens in library policy making.					
24.	Citizen participation must be sought for ALL library decisions, without restriction.					

25. Have opportunities (outside of the Library Board and Friends of the Library) for citizen participation in library policy making been created?

☐ No   ☐ Yes

Through the Model Cities Program
Through Office of Economic Opportunity Programs
Through other, NON-library initiated programs
    Explain_____

Through library initiated programs
    Explain_____

Don't know

IV. LIBRARY SERVICES:

26. Rank your library's service goal priorities. (Rank highest priority 1.)

☐ To enhance individual opportunities for self-development
☐ To aid in the creative use of leisure time
☐ To aid research
☐ To assist people in their daily occupations
☐ To provide information about community activities
☐ To provide and interpret library materials thus bringing materials
    and people together
☐ To increase ability in and enjoyment of reading
☐ To aid and supplement formal educational programs
☐ To provide the opportunity for the direct communication of ideas on
    important problems
☐ Other: (Specify)_____

27. Does the library as a whole or any of its branches in particular have specific library services or programs which you consider innovative?

☐ No   ☐ Yes (Describe briefly)_____
                    _____
                    _____
                    _____

28. Does the library maintain a file of community resources, activities or other community information?

☐ No   ☐ Yes (Explain purpose and use)_____
                    _____
                    _____
                    _____

29. During the past year, has the library received suggestions for new services which you think the library should <u>not</u> offer?

☐ No   ☐ Yes
                    Explain_____
                    _____
                    _____

30. Are other public or private non-library agencies presently offering services which you think are those that the library <u>should</u> be offering?

☐ No   ☐ Yes
                    Explain_____
                    _____
                    _____

31. Please make any additional comments which you believe would be relevant to the concerns of this study.

V. RESPONDENT IDENTIFICATION:

32. Name of library:_____.

33. Official title of your present position:_____.

34. Do you have a professional library degree; i.e., a M.S.L.S. or equivalent?

☐ No   ☐ Yes
                    From which school did you earn the degree?
                    _____.

35. How many years of library experience have you had?_____.

* THANK YOU *

Appendix C

CASE STUDY MATERIALS AND TECHNIQUES

The case study was undertaken in March 1972 and
was of six days' duration. Interviews were conducted with
28 persons at 10 locations throughout the city. Interview
responses were recorded at the time of the interview. The
persons interviewed were: 1) four of five top-level administrative staff members; 2) five of six library board members;
3) twelve professional staff members; 4) one pre-professional
staff member; 5) two non-professional staff members; 6) two
professional librarians residing in the city, but not employed
by the C. P. City Library; and 7) two representatives of library citizen groups. The interviews ranged in duration
from twenty minutes (with a non-professional staff member)
to several hours (with a member of the top-level administrative staff).

In addition to the interviews, clipping files maintained
by the C. P. City Library public relations department were
examined for the years 1968 to date. These files include,
in addition to all publicity developed by the library, all library-related items which appear in both city-wide and
neighborhood newspapers and magazines. Also, an extensive
history of the library and a recent master's degree level
paper on the library's outreach programs, plus a number of
political and sociological studies of the city were either read
in total or consulted for intelligence on particular concerns.

SELECTED BIBLIOGRAPHY

"The Access Study," Library Journal, 88 (December 15, 1963), 4685-4712.

Aiken, Michael, and others. The Structure of Community Power. New York: Random House, 1970.

Aleshire, Robert A. "Planning and Citizen Participation: Costs, Benefits and Approach," Urban Affairs Quarterly, 5 (June 1970), 369-393.

Altshuler, Alan A. Community Control; the Black Demand for Participation in Large American Cities. New York: Pegasus, 1970.

American Library Association. Public Library Association. A Strategy for Public Library Change: Proposed Public Library Goals--Feasibility Study, Allie Beth Martin, project coordinator. Chicago: American Library Association, 1972.

American Library Directory, 1968-1969. New York: Bowker, 1969.

Arnstein, Sherry R. "A Ladder of Citizen Participation." American Institute of Planners Journal, 35 (July 1969), 216-224.

Bachrach, Peter, and Baratz, Morton S. Power and Poverty; Theory and Practice. New York: Oxford University Press, 1970.

Banfield, Edward C. The Unheavenly City; the Nature and Future of Our Urban Crisis. Boston: Little, Brown, 1970.

_____, ed. Urban Government: Reader in Administration and Politics. Glencoe, Ill.: The Free Press, 1969.

_____ and Wilson, James Q. City Politics. New York: Vintage Books, 1963.

"Bargain Buy on Social Data," Behavior Today, 3 (January 17, 1972), 1.

Barss, Reitzel and Associates. Community Action and Institutional Change. Springfield, Va.: Clearinghouse for Scientific and Technical Information, July, 1969. (PB 185780).

Batchelder, Mildred L. Public Library Trustees in the Nineteen-Sixties. Chicago: American Library Association, 1969. (ALTA publication no. 4.)

Bauer, Raymond A. and Kenneth J. Gergen. The Study of Policy Formation. New York: The Free Press, 1968.

Baum, Bernard H. Decentralization of Authority in a Bureaucracy. Englewood Cliffs, N.J.: Prentice-Hall, 1961.

Beckman, Norman. "The Metropolitan Area: Coherence versus Chaos," Wilson Library Bulletin, 43 (January 1969), 438-443.

Bell, Daniel and Held, Virginia. "The Community Revolution," Public Interest, 16 (Summer 1969), 142-177.

Benson, Charles S. and Lund, Peter B. Neighborhood Distribution of Local Public Services. Berkeley: University of California Institute of Governmental Studies, 1969.

Berelson, Bernard. The Library's Public: A Report of the Public Library Inquiry. New York: Columbia University Press, 1949.

_____ and Steiner, Gary A. Human Behavior; An Inventory of Scientific Findings. New York: Harcourt, Brace & World, 1964.

Blankenship, L. Vaughn. "Community Power and Decision-making: A Comparative Evaluation of Measurement Techniques," Social Forces, 43 (October 1964), 207-216.

Blasingame, Ralph, ed. Research on Library Service in Metropolitan Areas: Report of a Rutgers Seminar 1964/65. New Brunswick, N.J.: Graduate School of Library Service, Rutgers--The State University, 1967.

Bone, Larry Earl. "Study in Renewal: A Library in Search of Itself," Library Journal, 97 (March 1, 1972), 844-847.

The Bowker Annual of Library and Book Trade Information, 1971. New York: Bowker, 1971.

Brandeis University. Florence Heller School for Advanced Studies in Social Welfare. Community Representation in Community Action Programs; Final Report (5). Springfield, Va.: Clearinghouse for Federal Scientific and Technical Information, March 1969. (PB 188 013)

Brown, Eleanor Frances. Modern Branch Libraries and Libraries in Systems. Metuchen, N.J.: Scarecrow, 1970.

Bundy, Mary Lee, ed. The Library's Public Revisited. College Park: University of Maryland, School of Library and Information Services, 1967.

_____. "Urban Information and Public Libraries: A Design for Service." Library Journal, 97 (January 15, 1972), 161-169.

_____ and Wasserman, Paul. The Public Library Administrator and His Situation; One Part of the Executive Study Portion of a Program of Research into the Identification of Manpower Requirements; the Educational Preparation and the Utilization of Manpower in the Library and Information Profession. College Park; University of Maryland. School of Library and Information Services, June, 1970.

Burke, Edmund M. "Citizen Participation Strategies," American Institute of Planners Journal, 34 (September

1968), 287-294.

Cartwright, Dorwin, ed. Studies in Social Power. Ann Ar-
bor: Institute for Social Research, 1959.

Chicago. University. Graduate Library School Conference,
32, 1967. The Public Library in the Urban Setting,
edited by Leon Carnovsky. Chicago: University of
Chicago Press, 1968.

"Citizen Participation in Model Cities, " Urban Data Service,
2 (July 1970).

"Citizen Participation in Urban Renewal, " Columbia Law Review, 66 (March 1966), 484-607.

Clark, Kenneth B. Dark Ghetto: Dilemmas of Social Power.
New York: Harper & Row, 1965.

_____. "A Role for Librarians in the Relevant War
Against Poverty, " Wilson Library Bulletin, 40 (September 1965), 42-47.

_____ and Hopkins, Jeanette. A Relevant War Against
Poverty; A Study of Community Action Programs and
Observable Social Change. New York: Harper &
Row, 1969.

Clark, Terry N., ed. Community Structure and Decision-
Making; Comparative Analyses. San Francisco:
Chandler, 1968.

_____. "Community Structure, Decision-Making, Budget
Expenditures and Urban Renewal in 51 American Communities, " American Sociological Review, 33 (August
1968), 576-93.

Clift, Virgil A. A Study of Library Services for the Disadvantaged in Buffalo, Rochester, and Syracuse. New
York: New York University, School of Education,
Center for Field Research and School Sources, June
1969. (ERIC LI 001 798)

Cloward, Richard A. "The War on Poverty; Are the Poor
Left Out?" The Nation, 201 (August 2, 1965), pp. 55-
60.

_____ and Ohlin, Lloyd E. Delinquency and Opportunity: A Theory of Delinquent Gangs. New York: Free Press, 1960.

Columbia University. School of Social Work. Neighborhood Information Centers; a Study and Some Proposals, by Alfred J. Kahn and others. New York: 1966.

Conant, Ralph W., ed. The Public Library and the City. Cambridge, Mass.: Massachusetts Institute of Technology Press, 1965.

"Current Trends in Branch Libraries, " Andrew Geddes, issue ed., Library Trends, 14 (April 1966).

"Current Trends in Urban Main Libraries, " Larry Earl Bone, issue ed., Library Trends, 20 (April 1972).

Dahl, Robert A. "The Concept of Power, " Behavioral Science, 2 (1959) 167-195.

Davis, James W. and Dolbeare, Kenneth M. "Citizen Participation in Government: Benchmarks for Policymakers" in Little Groups of Neighbors: The Selective Service System. Chicago: Markham, 1969, pp. 220-240.

Edelman, Murray. The Symbolic Uses of Politics. Urbana: University of Illinois Press, 1967.

Emerson, Richard M. "Power-Dependency Relations. " American Sociological Review, 27 (1962), 31-41.

Emory University. Division of Librarianship. Public Library Service to the Disadvantaged: Proceedings of an Institute, December 7-8, 1967. Atlanta, 1969.

Etzioni, Amitai. The Active Society. New York: Free Press, 1969.

Frederickson, H. George. Politics, Public Administration and Neighborhood Control. Los Angeles: Chandler, 1971.

Gans, Herbert J. The Urban Villagers: Group and Class in the Life of Italian Americans. New York: The Free Press, 1962.

164   Citizen Participation

Garceau, Oliver. The Public Library in the Political Pro-
    cess: A Report of the Public Library Inquiry. New
    York: Columbia University Press, 1949.

Gibson, Frank K. and Hawkins, Brett W. "Interviews ver-
    sus Questionnaires," American Behavioral Scientist,
    11 (September-October 1968), NS/9-NS/11.

Greenfield, Jeff and Newfield, Jack. A Populist Manifesto:
    The Making of a New Majority. New York: Praeger,
    1972.

Guthman, Judith Dommu. Metropolitan Libraries; The Chal-
    lenge and the Promise. Chicago: American Library
    Association, 1969. (The Public Library Reporter,
    15).

Hadden, Jeffrey K. and Borgatha, Edgar F. American Cities;
    Their Social Characteristics. Chicago: Rand
    McNally, 1965.

Hallman, Howard W. Administrative Decentralization and
    Citizen Control. Washington, D.C.: Center for Gov-
    ernmental Studies, 1971. (Pamphlet no. 7.)

_____. Community Control: a Study of Community Cor-
    porations and Neighborhood Boards. Washington,
    D.C.: Washington Center for Metropolitan Studies,
    1969.

Hamburg, Morris and others. A Systems Analysis of the
    Library and Information Science Statistical Data Sys-
    tem: The Research Investigation. Philadelphia:
    University of Pennsylvania, June 1970.

Hanson, Royce. The Political Thicket. Englewood Cliffs,
    N.J.: Prentice-Hall, 1966.

Harrington, Michael. The Other America. New York:
    Macmillan, 1962.

_____. "An Unconditional War," Wilson Library Bulletin,
    38, (June 1964), 835-39.

Hawley, Willis D. and Wirt, Frederick M., eds. The
    Search for Community Power. Englewood Cliffs,
    N.J.: Prentice-Hall, 1968.

Hirsch, Werner Z. "The Supply of Urban Public Services, "
in Harvey S. Perloff & Lowdon Wingo Jr. (eds.)
Issues in Urban Economics. Baltimore: Johns Hopkins University Press, 1968.

HUD News, March 26, 1970.

Hunter, Floyd. Community Power Structure. Chapel Hill:
University of North Carolina Press, 1953.

Joeckel, Carleton B. Government of the American Public
Library. Chicago: University of Chicago Press,
1935.

Johnson, Gerald W. "Role of the Public Library, " in American Library Association, Public Library Service.
Chicago: American Library Association, 1956.

Kaufman, Herbert. Administrative Decentralization and Political Power; Paper given at 1968 Annual meeting
of the American Political Science Association, Washington, D. C.

Keller, Suzanne Infeld. The Urban Neighborhood: a Sociological Perspective. New York: Random House,
1968.

Kerlinger, Fred N. Foundations of Behavioral Research.
New York: Holt, Rinehart and Winston, 1964.

Koepp, Donald W. Decision-making for the Public Library
Function of Municipal Government. Berkeley, University of California, 1966. (Ph. D. dissertation).

_____. "The Library Board in City Government; An an-
achronism?" Bulletin of the Institute of Government
Studies, 8 (October 1967), unpaged.

Kotz, Nick. "End of Programs Run by Poor Foreseen Under
Nixon Proposal, " The Washington Post, 94, (May 3,
1971) Section A, 1-2.

Kramer, Ralph. Participation of the Poor. Englewood
Cliffs, N. J.: Prentice-Hall, 1969.

Krause, Elliott A. "Functions of a Bureaucratic Ideology:
Citizen Participation, " Social Problems, 16 (Fall

1968), 129-143.

Kroll, Morton. Public Libraries of the Pacific Northwest.
Seattle: University of Washington Press, 1960.

Lammers, C. J. "Power and Participation in Decision-
making in Formal Organizations," American Journal
of Sociology, 73 (September 1967), 201-216.

Langton, Kenneth P. Political Socialization. New York:
Oxford University Press, 1969.

Lasswell, Harold D. and Kaplau, Abraham. Power and Society. New Haven: Yale University Press, 1950.

Lewis, Hylan. "Culture, Class and Family Life Among Low-
Income Urban Negroes." Arthur M. Ross and Her-
bert Hill (eds.) Employment, Race and Poverty.
New York: Harcourt, Brace and World, 1967.

Lewis, Oscar. Five Families. New York: Basic Books,
1959.

"Library Outreach," Wilson Library Bulletin, 43, May 1969,
848-903.

Liebow, Elliott. Tally's Corner. Boston: Little, Brown,
1967.

Likert, Ransis. The Human Organization: Its Management
and Value. New York: McGraw-Hill, 1967.

Lindblom, Charles E. The Policy making Process. Englewood Cliffs, N.J.: Prentice-Hall, 1968.

Lineberry, Robert L. and Sharkansky, Ira. Urban Politics
and Public Policy. New York: Harper & Row, 1971.

Lipsky, Michael. "Protest as a Political Resource," American Political Science Review, 62 (September 1968),
1144-1158.

_____. Toward a Theory of Street-Level Bureaucracy.
Paper prepared for presentation at the 1969 Annual
meeting of the American Political Science Association, New York. September 2-6, 1969. New York:
American Political Science Association, 1969.

Lipsman, Claire. Library Service to the Disadvantaged.
    1971. (Unpublished manuscript).

Lowin, Aaron. "Participative Decision-Making: Model,
    Literature Critique, and prescriptions for Research, "
    Organizational Behavior and Human Performance, 3
    (1968), 68-106.

Lowry, Ritchie P. Who's Running This Town? Community
    Leadership and Social Changes. New York: Harper
    and Row, 1962.

McCleery, Richard. "Communication Patterns as Bases of
    Systems of Authority and Power, " in Theoretical
    Studies in Social Organization of the Prison. New
    York: Social Science Research Council, 1960.

Marcuse, Herbert. An Essay on Liberation. Boston: Bea-
    con, 1969.

Margolis, Julius. "The Demand for Urban Services, " in
    Harvey S. Perloff and Lowdon Wingo Jr. (eds.)
    Issues in Urban Economics. Baltimore: Johns Hop-
    kins University Press, 1968.

Marris, Peter and Rein, Martin. Dilemmas of Social Re-
    form; Poverty and Community Action with the U.S.
    New York: Atherton, 1969.

Marrow, A. J., Seashore, S. E., and Bowers, D. G.
    Management by Participation. New York: Harper &
    Row, 1968.

Martin, Lowell. Library Response to Urban Change. Chi-
    cago: American Library Association, 1969.

Massarik, and Tannenbaum. "Participation by Subordinates
    in the Management Decision-making Process, " Canad-
    ian Journal of Economics and Political Science, 16
    (August 1950), 408-418.

Mead, Margaret and Brown, Muriel. The Wagon and the
    Star; a Study of American Community Initiative. Chi-
    cago: Rand McNally, 1966.

Merelman, Richard M. "On the Neo-Elitist Critique of
    Community Power, " American Political Science Re-

view, 62 (June 1968), 451-460.

"The Metropolitan Public Library, " Wilson Library Bulletin,
    40 (June 1966), 917-929.

Milbrath, Lester W. Political Participation. Chicago:
    Rand McNally, 1965.

Miller, Abraham H. Information and Change: Requirements
    for Urban Decision Making. Davis: University of
    California, Institute of Government Affairs, 1970.

Miller, S. M. Breaking the Credentials Barrier; an address
    delivered before the American Orthopsychiatric Asso-
    ciation, Washington, D.C., March 23, 1967. New
    York, Ford Foundation, 1967. (A Ford Foundation
    Reprint, SR/26.)

_____ and Rein, Martin. "Participation, Poverty and Ad-
    ministration, " Public Administration Review, 29 (Jan-
    uary-February 1969), 15-25.

Mills, C. Wright. Power, Politics, and People. Fair
    Lawn, N.J.: Oxford University Press, 1969.

Monat, William R. The Public Library and its Community;
    A Study of the Impact of Library Services in Five
    Pennsylvania Cities. State College: Pennsylvania
    State University, Institute of Public Administration,
    1967.

Mouzelis, Nicos P. Organisation and Bureaucracy. Chicago:
    Aldine, 1968.

Moynihan, Daniel P. Maximum Feasible Misunderstanding.
    New York: Free Press, 1969.

Mulder, Mauk. "Power Equalization through Participation, "
    Administration Science Quarterly, 16 (March 1971),
    31-38.

National Education Resources Institute. A Systems Analysis
    of Southwestern Spanish speaking Users and Nonusers
    of Library and Information Services, Developing Cri-
    teria to Design an Optimal Library Model Concept;
    progress report II. Washington: 1970.

National Federation of Settlements and Neighborhood Centers.
    Local Community Structure and Civic Participation;
    Report of study conducted under contract with the Na-
    tional Commission on Urban Problems.   Chicago:
    1968.

New York (State) Library.   Extension Division.   Conference
    on Library Participation in Antipoverty Programs,
    Thayer Hotel, Westpoint, February 7-9, 1966.   Pro-
    ceedings.   Albany: 1966.

Nisbett, Robert A.   Community and Power.   Fair Lawn,
    N. J.:   Oxford University Press, 1962.

Olson, Edwin E.   Interlibrary Cooperation.   Washington,
    D. C.:   U. S. Office of Education, Bureau of Research,
    1970 (ERIC ED 046421).

_____.   Survey of the User Service Policies in Indiana
    Libraries and Information Centers.   Indiana Library
    Studies, Report 10, 1970.   (ERIC EDO44139).

Orden, Susan R. and others.   Community Action Programs
    as Agents of Change in the Private Welfare Sector.
    Springfield, Va.:   Clearinghouse of Scientific and
    Technical Information, August 1969.   (PB 185 782).

Peabody, Robert L.   Organizational Authority; Superior-Sub-
    ordinate Relationships in Three Public Service Organi-
    zations.   New York: Atherton Press, 1964.

Penland, Patrick R.   Floating Librarians in the Community:
    Report of the Institute on the Floating Librarian in
    the Emerging Community July 13-31, 1970 at the
    Graduate School of Library and Information Sciences,
    University of Pittsburgh, Pittsburgh, 1970.

Perrow, Charles.   Organizational Analysis; a Sociological
    View.   Belmont, California: Wadsworth, 1970.

Peterson, Paul E.   "Forms of Representation: Participa-
    tion of the Poor in the Community Action Program."
    American Political Science Review, 64 (June 1970),
    451-507.

Piven, Frances.   "Participation of Residents in Neighbor-
    hood Community Action Programs."   Social Work, 21

(January 1966), 73-80.

_____. "Resident Participation in Community Action Pro-
grams: An Overview," in Brager, G. A. and Pur-
cell, F. P., eds. Community Action Against Poverty. New Haven: Community College and University
Press, 1967.

Polsby, Nelson W. Community Power and Political Theory.
New Haven, Conn.: Yale University Press, 1963.

Public Administration and Neighborhood Control; Proceedings
of a Conference held in Boulder, Colorado, May 6-8,
1970. Washington, D. C.: Center for Governmental
Studies, 1970.

Public Library Association, PLA Newsletter, 11 (Spring
1972).

The Rand Corporation. A Million Random Digits. Glencoe,
Ill.: Free Press, 1955.

Riessman, Frank. The Culturally Deprived Child. New
York: Harper and Row, 1962.

Rossi, Peter H. "Power and Community Structure," Mid-
west Journal of Political Science, 4 (November 1960),
390-401.

Rothman, Jack. "An Analysis of Goals and Roles in Community Organization Practice." Social Work, 19
(April 1964), 24-31.

Sayre, Wallace S. and Herbert Kaufman. Governing New
York City. New York: Norton, 1972.

Schattschneider, E. E. The Semisovereign People. New
York: Holt, Rinehart and Winston, 1960.

Schick, Frank L. Board-librarian Relations in American
Public Libraries. Chicago: University of Chicago,
1948. Thesis (M. S.).

Schmandt, Henry J. Decentralization: A Structural Impera-
tive. Washington, D. C.: Center for Governmental
Studies, May 1970. (mimeographed paper)

Schwartz, Jerome L. and Cherin, Milton. "Participation of
    Recipients in Public Welfare Planning and Administra-
    tion," Social Work 21 (January 1966), 10-22.

Selltiz, Claire and others. Research Methods in Social Re-
    lations. Rev. one vol. ed. New York: Holt, Rine-
    hart & Winston, 1959.

Sharkansky, Ira. Regionalism in American Politics. Indian-
    apolis: Bobbs-Merrill, 1970.

_____, ed. Policy Analysis in Political Science. Chi-
    cago: Markham, 1970.

Shostak, Arthur B. "Promoting Participation of the Poor;
    Philadelphia's Antipoverty Program," Social Work,
    21 (January 1966), 64-71.

Snedecor, George W. and Cochran, William G. Statistical
    Methods. Ames, Iowa: Iowa University Press, 1967.

Spiegel, Hans B. C., ed. Citizen Participation in Urban
    Development. Washington, D.C.: National Training
    Laboratories Institute for Applied Behavioral Science,
    1968.

_____ and Mittenthal, Stephen D., Neighborhood Power
    and Control; Implications for Urban Planning. Spring-
    field, Va.: Clearinghouse for Scientific and Technical
    Information, November 1968 (PB 183176).

Stiebar, Jack. "Employee Representation in Municipal Gov-
    ernment," in Municipal Year Book, 1969. Washing-
    ton, D.C.; International City Management Association,
    1969, p. 3-57.

Swanson, Bert E., ed. Current trends in Comparative Com-
    munity Studies. Kansas City, Mo.: Community
    Studies, Inc., 1962.

Theobald, Robert. "Policy Formation for New Goals," in
    Robert Theobald (ed.) Social Policies for America in
    the Seventies. Garden City, N.Y.: Doubleday, 1968.

U.S. Bureau of the Census. County and City Data Book,
    1967. Washington, D.C.: Government Printing Of-
    fice, 1968.

U.S. Department of Housing and Urban Development. Citizen Participation in Model Cities; A HUD Guide. Washington, D.C.: 1968. (Technical Assistance Bulletin, 3).

    . "Internal Memo on Library Programs in Model Cities." Washington, D.C.: October, 1970. (Unpublished.)

    . The Model Cities Program; A History and Analysis of the Planning Process in Three Cities: Atlanta, Georgia, Seattle, Washington, Dayton, Ohio. Washington, D.C.: Government Printing Office, 1969.

U.S. Department of Justice. Community Relations Service. Citizen Participation: An Analytical Study of the Literature by Vincent Mathews. Washington, D.C.: 1968.

U.S. Laws, Statutes, etc. Demonstration Cities and Metropolitan Development Act of 1966. Public Law 89-754. Washington, D.C.: Government Printing Office, 1966.

    . Economic Opportunity Act of 1964. Public Law 88-452. Washington, D.C.: Government Printing Office, 1964.

U.S. Office of Economic Opportunity. Community Action Agency Atlas, 3rd ed. Washington, D.C.: May 1971. (OEO Manual 6003-1B.)

U.S. Office of Education. Statistics of Libraries: An Annotated Bibliography of Recurring Surveys, by John C. Rather. Washington, D.C.: 1961 (USOE publication no. 15022).

    . Library Services Branch. Statistics or Public Libraries Serving Areas with at Least 25,000 Inhabitants. Washington, D.C.: 1968.

Valentine, Charles. Culture and Poverty. Chicago: University of Chicago Press, 1968.

Vanecko, James J. Community Mobilization and Institutional Change: The Influence of the Community Action Program in Large Cities. Chicago: National Opinion Research Center, 1970. (NORC Reprint.)

Voos, Henry. Information Needs in Urban Areas. New
    Brunswick, N. J.: Rutgers University Press, 1969.

Washnis, George J. "Municipal Decentralization: Little
    City Halls and Other Neighborhood Facilities." in
    Municipal Yearbook, 1971, Washington, D.C.: Inter-
    national City Management Association, 1971, p. 8-12.

_____. Neighborhood Facilities and Municipal Decentrali-
    zation, v. 1. Comparative Analysis of Twelve Cities.
    Washington, D.C.: Center for Governmental Studies,
    March 1971.

Westby, David L. "The War on Poverty in the Urban Com-
    munity: A Social and Political Analysis. Pennsyl-
    vania State. University, Institute of Public Adminis-
    tration, 1970. (Manuscript.)

"Who Participates in What?" A Bibliographic Essay on In-
    dividual Participation in Urban Areas." Urban Affairs
    Quarterly, 3 (December 1968), 201-224.

Williams, Oliver P. "Life Style Values and Political De-
    centralization in Metropolitan Areas," Southwestern
    Social Science Quarterly, 48 (December 1962), 299-
    310.

Wilson, James Q., "Planning and Politics: Citizen Partici-
    pation in Urban Renewal." American Institute of
    Planners Journal, 29 (November 1963), 242-249.

_____, ed. City Politics and Public Policy. New York:
    Wiley, 1968.

Winsor, Charlotte B. A Study of Four Library Programs
    for Disadvantaged Persons. Albany: New York State
    Library, 1967.

Wood, Robert C. "A Call for Return to Community."
    Public Management, 8 (July 1969), 2-9.

_____. "When Government Works." The Public Interest,
    no. 18 (Winter 1970), 39-51.

Yamane, Taro. Elementary Sampling Theory. Englewood
    Cliffs, N. J.: Prentice-Hall, 1967.

Young, Virginia G. The Library Trustee; A Practical Guide
     book. New York: Bowker, 1969.

INDEX

DATE DUE			
APR 13 '78			
MAY 4 '78			
APR 14 '81			
AUG 6 '81			
GAYLORD			PRINTED IN U.S.A.